COLLINS GEM

MU...
&TOADSTOOLS
PHOTOGUIDE

D0498735

Text by Patrick Harding
Photographs by Alan Outen

HarperCollins*Publishers*

HarperCollins*Publishers*
PO Box, Glasgow G4 0NB
First published 1996

Reprint 9 8 7 6 5 4 3 2 1 0

ISBN 0 00 470934 9

Typeset by TJ Graphics

Printed in Italy by Amadeus S.p.A

INTRODUCTION

Mushrooms and toadstools belong to the fungi kingdom. There are about 4,000 species of larger fungi in Britain. Of the larger umbrella-shaped fungi with a cap and stem, mushroom is a popular term for those that are edible; toadstool for those that are poisonous.

A fungus is not a plant. Most plants make food using the sun's energy. Animals and fungi need a food source, usually plant or animal, living or dead. Animals digest food internally. In fungi enzymes dissolve the food externally from where it is absorbed.

Plants and animals are made up of many tiny cells, but mushrooms and toadstools are composed of very thin tubes known as hyphae. As a hypha grows it branches and produces a web of threads known as a mycelium. This is the equivalent of stems, roots and leaves in a plant. On a flat surface it often grows as an expanding disc and this shape is clearly seen in simple fungi such as moulds on food.

Unlike moulds, mushrooms and toadstools reproduce by forming spores in large fruitbodies. These are the structures that are described in this book and frequently the rest of the fungus is hidden from view. A fruitbody may only exist for a few days before rotting away but the mycelium which produces it may live for years and some individuals are known to be hundreds of years old.

WHERE DO FUNGI GROW?

Many species described in this book are found among short mown or grazed grass. Such fungi feed on dead plant or animal material present in the soil. Undisturbed pasture that has not been ploughed or had chemical fertilisers applied is usually much richer in fungi than reseeded grass which has been limed and fertilised.

Lawns and playing fields are often carefully prepared, with the soil being riddled to remove stones and as such provide perfect sites for the growth of 'fairy rings' - the appearance of a ring of fruitbodies. In the past these were explained away by references to toads or fairies but they result from fruitbodies being produced at the growing edge of the buried mycelium which under uniform soil conditions grows as a circular disc. As the mycelium grows so the size of the circle increases.

Grazed grassland attracts species of fungi that feed on dung. Horse and cow dung is especially rich in fungi though many have small fruitbodies. Larger species include Dung Roundhead (p.119) and Egg-shell Toadstool (p.148).

Woodlands are home to a wide range of fungi. In addition to species growing in woodland soil there are those that rot tree leaves (and conifer needles), those that rot fallen wood and old stumps and those that feed on living trees. Of the latter some enter as germinating spores through a wound and the mycelium spreads before producing bracket-like fruitbodies from the trunk. Others invade via the tree roots and form a web or mycorrhiza (fungus root). Such fungi draw food from tree roots but produce terrestrial fruitbodies though some (e.g. truffles) produce them underground.

Many species are restricted to one or a small number of tree species. Jelly Antler Fungus (p.209) grows on pine stumps and also on spruce. Hen of the Woods (p.200) is only found at the base of oak trees. Mycorrhizal species are especially host specific and their names often relate to this, e.g. Brown Birch Bolete (p.160) and Beechwood Sickener (p.86). Some tree species have a large number of associated species of fungi and among those with the most are oak, beech, birch and Scots pine.

Other habitats include gardens and parks. More specific places include cellars, wood stacks, old bonfire sites and manure heaps. Some fungi, e.g. Ergot (p.241), grow from grass flowers while others emerge from the bodies of animals they have killed.

Edible and Poisonous Fungi

Many edible fungi have 'lookalikes' which may be poisonous. This is even true for the Field Mushroom, the most commonly consumed wild fungus in Britain. Beginners must on no account gather wild fungi to eat unless they have been correctly identified by an expert. Before eating wild fungi consult *How to Identify Edible Mushrooms* by Harding, Lyon and Tomblin, published by HarperCollins.

Some fungi cannot be identified without a microscope but most of the species in this book can be named using macro characters. Collect the whole fungus (using a knife if necessary) and place in a basket. Fragile species are best put in small boxes. Make notes about habitat, e.g. 'growing on a stump' or 'under birch' and remember that a slimy texture or faint smell may dry or fade.

In this book descriptions concentrate on characters of the fruitbody, including colour (which is very variable), shape (which often changes as the fruitbody matures - NB a raised central region is known as an umbo), smell and texture. Most species are umbrella- or mushroom-shaped and have gills on the cap underside, like shop mushrooms.

Gill characters are important, especially the way they are attached to the stem. This is best seen by slicing the cap in half.

Gill Characteristics

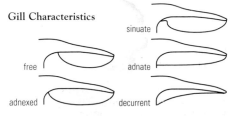

A spore print (the colour of a mass of spores) is very important for accurate identification. Remove stem and put the cap gills (or tubes) down on a piece of glass. Cover to keep moist and leave for at least 4 hours, after which there be a white or coloured deposit.

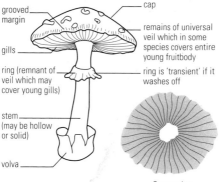

grooved margin

cap

remains of universal veil which in some species covers entire young fruitbody

gills

ring (remnant of veil which may cover young gills)

ring is 'transient' if it washes off

stem (may be hollow or solid)

volva

Spore print

Species entries
The information provided is arranged as follows:

- A symbol – see p.3 for explanation
- The Family or group to which the species belongs.
- The Spore Colour of the species.
- The English Name of the species. In some cases where there is more than one English name in common usage an alternative is mentioned.

7

- The Latin Name of the species. As with flowering plants this binomial is printed in italics. The first part of the name is the genus to which it belongs. The second part is the species name. As with other organisms Latin names can change, especially as modern research improves our knowledge of the relationship between species. Where there have been recent changes the former Latin name is also given.
- The main paragraph gives background details and lists the most important features to aid identification. Features are described in order: cap, gills (where present) and stem. Features that cannot be shown in the photograph such as texture and smell are also listed here.

Size	This gives the normal range. The measures are (usually) for cap diameter, stem height and stem width.
Habitat	An important section as some fungi are only found in very restricted habitats.
Season	This gives the usual fruiting season but remember that unusual weather conditions may cause fruitbodies to appear at odd times.
Poisonous	Edible, Inedible, Poisonous (red = Very poisonous) An indication of possible culinary use is given but beginners should avoid gathering and eating wild fungi without an expert having identified them first.
Similar species	This section includes both closely related species (usually in the same genus) and species which look similar and may confuse a beginner.

KEY TO SPECIES ILLUSTRATED IN THE BOOK

At each number there is a range of alternative descriptions
- choose that which most closely fits your specimen. This
will direct you to the next key stage or to a page number.

1 FRUITBODY SHAPE

    a Grows on wood like a crust, shelf or bracket
       with no stem or a laterally attached stem   **see 2**

    b Finger, club, antler or coral shape   **see 3**

    c Spherical, star or nest shape   **see 4**

    d Ear, saddle, brain or cauliflower shape   **see 5**

    e Disc, saucer or cup shape   **see 6**

    f Umbrella shape with cap and central stem   **see 7**

2 CRUST, SHELF OR BRACKET-LIKE

    a Gills on the underside 109, 165, 170-173

    b Smooth underside;   181-183
       bracket < 7cm across, < 1cm thick

    c Tiny pores or folds underneath; 184-187
       bracket < 7cm across, < 1cm thick

    d Round, angular or slit-like pores; 188-200
       bracket >7cm across, >1cm thick

3 FINGER, CLUB, ANTLER OR CORAL SHAPE

    a Jelly-like texture   207-209

    b Brittle or hard texture   **see c or d**

    c Unbranched, finger or club shape
       1 Brittle texture 174, 220-221, 239-241
       2 Hard texture   244-245

    d Branched, antler or coral shape
       1 Brittle texture   175-177
       2 Hard texture   244

4 SPHERICAL, STAR OR NEST SHAPE

a Skin peeling back, star-like   223

b Nest-like with tiny 'eggs'   224

c Spherical; > 1.5 cm diameter

    1 Growing on birch, tough, white   192

    2 Thin skin, white flesh   210-218

    3 Thick skin, dark flesh   219-220

    4 Jelly layer below skin   221-222

    5 Underground fruitbody   242-243

    6 On trees, hard, brown-black   246

d Spherical; < 0.5cm diameter 206, 247-248

5 EAR, SADDLE OR BRAIN SHAPE

a Ear shape (jelly-like)   203

b Brain shape (jelly-like)   204-205

c Brain shape (dry texture)   233-234

d Saddle shape (dry texture)   231-232

6 DISC, SAUCER OR CUP SHAPE

a Jelly-like texture   203, 236-238

b Dry texture   180, 225-230

7 UMBRELLA SHAPE WITH CENTRALLY ATTACHED STEM CAP WITH:

a Teeth on underside   178-179

b Pores on underside   150-163, 201-202

c Smooth or wrinkled underside 167-169, 235

d Gills on underside   **see 8**

8 MUSHROOMS AND TOADSTOOLS WITH GILLS
SPORE COLOUR:

    a *Pink* ●

      1 Gills free, on rotting wood   101-102

      2 Gills not free   103-109

    b *Brown* ● ● ●

      1 In grass, small and fragile   110-111, 131

      2 In grass, medium sized, with ring   112

      3 Woodland species   121-130

    c *Brown* ● ● ●

      1 Gills free   132-136

      2 Gills not free   113-120, 164

    d *Black* ●

      1 Inky fluid from old gills   137-142

      2 No inky fluid, plain gills   143-145

      3 No inky fluid, mottled gills   146-149

    e *White* (or very pale colour) ○   **see 9**

9 MUSHROOMS AND TOADSTOOLS WITH WHITE SPORES
(including cream and pale yellow)

    a Gills free

      1 Volva at stem base   13-20

      2 No volva, ring on stem   21-23

      Gills not free   **see b**

    b Gills thick, waxy, mostly in grass   66-73

      Gills not thick and waxy   **see c**

  c Fruitbody easily crumbled, woodland spp

see d

  Fruitbody not easily crumbled   **see e**

  d No milky fluid from damaged gills 74-88

  Damaged gills exude milky fluid 89-100

  e Ring present on stem   24, 53, 55-56

  Ring absent   **see f**

  f Bell-shaped cap, slender stem   42-49

  Convex, flat or funnel-shaped cap **see g**

  g Gills decurrent   25-26, 29-33,

50-51, 166

  Gills sinuate   27-28, 57-62, 64-65

  Gills adnate or adnexed   **see h**

  h Cap < 1.5cm, on twigs, leaves or needles

40-41

  Cap > 1.5cm across   **see i**

  i Stem pliable, not easily broken

34-39, 52, 54

  Stem not pliable, easily broken   63

FLY AGARIC *Amanita muscaria*

A striking, commonly found fungus often depicted in fairy tale illustrations and on greeting cards. It was traditionally used as a fly killer. The entire young fruitbody is enclosed in a white veil which leaves fragments (which may wash off) on the shiny red, marginally grooved cap. The gills are white and free, the ring hanging and grooved. The stem base is swollen with rings of scales (remains of volva).

Size	Cap 10-20 cm, stem 15-20 cm x 15-20 mm.
Habitat	Mostly with birch; also with pine and spruce.
Season	Late summer to early winter.
Poisonous	Rarely fatal. Hallucinogenic properties.
Similar species	The edible Caesar's Mushroom (*A.caesarea*) has an orange-red, mostly unspotted cap, yellow stem and gills and a sack-like volva. Not found in Britain.

PANTHER CAP *Amanita pantherina*

Uncommon but often confused with Tall Amanita (p.15), its ochre-brown cap has a grooved margin and regular pattern of white, warty veil fragments (these may wash off). The gills are white and free, the ring ungrooved and pendulous. The white stem has several scaly rings above the eggcup-like swollen base.

Size	Cap 5-10 cm, stem 6-10 cm x 10-20 mm.
Habitat	Broad-leaved and coniferous woods.
Season	Summer to autumn.
Poisonous	Can be fatal if consumed.
Similar species	Tall Amanita (p.15) differs in its grey cap spots, less obvious volva and grooves on the upper surface of the ring. The Blusher (p.16) also has ring grooves and a less obvious volva but flesh-coloured cap spots.

TALL AMANITA *Amanita excelsa*

The flat grey-brown cap is covered with irregular pale grey patches from the remains of the veil which enclosed the young fruitbody. The gills are free and white. The stem is white with a white transient ring which is grooved on the upper surface. The swollen base has bands of scales but no enclosing sack.

Size	Cap 10-15 cm, stem 10-12 cm x 10-20 mm.
Habitat	Broad-leaved and coniferous woods.
Season	Summer to early autumn.
Poisonous	Easily confused with poisonous species and so not recommended.
Similar species	Panther Cap (p.14) differs in its white cap patches, ungrooved ring and rimmed top to the swollen stem base.

15

THE BLUSHER *Amanita rubescens*

The rounded cap is initially covered with the off-white veil which leaves remnants on the flatter, older cap. The remnants are grey, flesh-coloured or pale yellow and are later widely spaced, if present at all. The underlying cap colour ranges from cream to dark brown. The white gills and flesh bruise pinky-red. The broad white stem has a bulbous base and is flecked rosy-brown below the white, grooved ring.

Size	Cap 5-15 cm, stem 7-15 cm x 10-25 mm.
Habitat	Broad-leaved and coniferous woods.
Season	Early summer to autumn.
Edible	Must be well cooked. Causes anaemia if eaten raw.
Similar species	Confused with Panther Cap, Tall Amanita and Death Cap (pp.14, 15 & 17) none of which turn pinky-red on bruising or cutting.

DEATH CAP *Amanita phalloides*

One of the most poisonous of all fungi; it has caused many fatalities. After bursting through the white veil the shiny, olive-yellow to greeny-bronze flattened cap is usually devoid of veil fragments. The gills are white and crowded, the white ring grooved and pendulous. The white stem has faint, wavy cap-coloured zones. The base is encased in a white, sack-like volva. It has an unpleasant smell when old.

Size	Cap 5-12 cm, stem 10-12 cm x 10-20 mm.
Habitat	Broad-leaved woods, especially with oak or beech.
Season	Midsummer to late autumn.
Poisonous	Causes liver and kidney failure.
Similar species	Confused with False Death Cap (p.18) which is paler, has no sack-like volva and smells strongly of radish.

17

FALSE DEATH CAP *Amanita citrina*

The cap is pale lemon with irregular ochre-yellow veil fragments. Also common as a white form (var. *alba*). The gills are white and free. The stem is paler than the cap, with a white ring grooved on the upper surface, as is the stem apex. There is a trough-like volva at the bulbous stem base. It smells of raw potato or radish.

Size	Cap 4-9 cm, stem 5-7 cm x 10-15 mm.
Habitat	In both coniferous and broad-leaved woods, mostly with beech.
Season	Midsummer to autumn.
Edible	Not recommended as too easily confused with poisonous species (see opposite).
Similar species	Death Cap (p.17) is darker; Destroying Angel (p.19) is whiter; both lack the sharp smell.

DESTROYING ANGEL *Amanita virosa*

The cap is initially hidden in the white veil which is cast off to reveal a smooth, slightly sticky, bell-shaped cap with crowded, white, free gills. The slender white, often curved stem bears loose scales and a large transient ring just below the cap. The base is enclosed in a white sack-like volva. It has a sickly sweet smell.

Size	Cap 5-10 cm, stem 10-15 cm x 10-15 mm.
Habitat	With broad-leaved trees, especially birch.
Season	Late summer to autumn.
Poisonous	Symptoms like those from Death Cap.
Similar species	The pale form of False Death Cap (p.18) lacks the sack-like volva. Mushrooms (pp.132–136) lack a volva and have pink gills with dark brown spores.

Tawny Grisette *Amanita fulva*

Unlike other ·common Amanitas, this and the similar, less common, grey-capped Grisette have no ring. Expanding through a white veil, the shiny cap (sticky when moist) is orange-brown with a darker, raised centre and grooved margin. It has white, free gills. The smooth white stem is flushed with the cap colour and narrows towards the apex. The white sack-like volva encloses the stem base.

Size	Cap 4-8 cm, stem 10-15 cm x 10-15 mm.
Habitat	Broad-leaved woods.
Season	Midsummer to autumn.
Edible	Must be well cooked. Not recommended.
Similar species	Grisette (*A. vaginata*) is slightly larger and has a grey to grey-brown cap.

PARASOL MUSHROOM *Macrolepiota procera*

When young, it is shaped like an egg on a stick but the mature cap is flat apart from a raised, dark brown central region which is surrounded by rings of flat brown scales on a cream background. It has dry, creamy-white gills. The long hollow stem tapers from a swollen base and bears faint snake-like markings below the movable double ring.

Size	Cap 10-25 cm, stem 15-35 cm x 15-25 mm.
Habitat	Meadows, parks, roadside verges, open woodland.
Season	Midsummer to late autumn.
Edible	Excellent nutty taste. Discard stem and fry the cap whole, coated in breadcrumbs.
Similar species	Often confused with Shaggy Parasol (p.22). Slender Parasol (*M. gracilenta*) is about half the size and lacks scales at the cap edge.

SHAGGY PARASOL *Macrolepiota rhacodes*

Frequently confused with Parasol Mushroom, it is smaller, stockier and has a more convex, fleshier cap covered with pale beige scales which bend away from the cap. The white stem bruises red-brown. The cap and stem flesh, together with the cream-coloured gills, turn orange-red when cut. It has a strong, slightly sweet smell.

Size Cap 12-18 cm, stem 8-12 cm x 15-20 mm.
Habitat In grass with trees and near garden compost.
Season Midsummer to late autumn.
Edible A minority suffer from digestive upset and skin rash.
Similar species Variety *hortensis* is stockier with chestnut-coloured scales. *M.konradii* is smaller with a smoother brown cap and only very slight flesh reddening.

STINKING PARASOL *Lepiota cristata*

The small bell-shaped cap matures flat but with a
raised red-brown centre surrounded by rings of
small, similar-coloured scales on a pinky-white
ground. The very crowded, free white gills age
browner. The slender silky white stem bears a small
transient ring. Unpleasant smell of rubber or tar.

Size	Cap 2-5 cm, stem 3-6 cm x 3-4 mm.
Habitat	In lawns and pastures and among woodland litter.
Season	Late summer to autumn.
Poisonous	Many closely related species are very poisonous so do not eat small 'Parasols'.
Similar species	Less common species include those with white, olive or dark-brown cap-scales and those with a fruity smell. Some are very poisonous.

SAFFRON PARASOL *Cystoderma amianthinum*

Similar to the small Lepiotas, e.g. Stinking Parasol (p.23), but with gills attached to the stem. The thin-fleshed, ochre-yellow cap has a granular surface and a shaggy edge. It has adnate, creamy-white gills. The slender, cap-coloured stem is unusual in that the lower region (below the shaggy, often incomplete ring) is covered with tiny scales. It has an earthy smell.

Size	Cap 2-5 cm, stem 4-7 cm x 3-4 mm.
Habitat	Among moss and grass in acid pastures and heaths. Also with needle litter in coniferous woods.
Season	Late summer to autumn.
Inedible	Not worthwhile.
Similar species	*C. carcharias* is pinky-grey and is commonest under pine or spruce.

The Deceiver *Laccaria laccata*

A common woodland species often occuring in large troops. The cap is flat or slightly depressed, pinky-brown, drying paler. It has a granular central region and a striate edge when moist. The gills are flesh-coloured, adnate to slightly decurrent, thick and widely spaced. The stem is thin, fibrous and often flattened.

Size	Cap 1-4 cm, stem 3-10 cm x 2-5 mm.
Habitat	Among tree leaf litter and on heaths.
Season	Late summer to autumn.
Edible	Lacking in flavour. Discard the tough stems.
Similar species	Closely related species include the larger *L.proxima* growing on peaty soil and the paler *L.bicolor* with a lilac stem base. Tough Shanks (pp.35 to 38) have crowded gills.

AMETHYST DECEIVER *Laccaria amethystea*

Often found in large troops. When young and moist, the cap, stem and gills are deep violet. The cap and stem mature pale buff, the widely-spaced gills to white. The cap edge is often wavy or split, the centre is slightly rough and often darker. The tough stem is frequently bent or twisted.

Size	Cap 1-4 cm, stem 4-8 cm x 3-6 mm.
Habitat	With conifers and broad-leaved trees, mostly among beech litter.
Season	Autumn or late summer to early winter.
Edible	Retains its colour when cooked but lacks flavour.
Similar species	The Deceiver (p.25) is similar but is red-brown. Lilac Bell Cap (p.47) is rosy-lilac with grey-tinged gills and smells of radish. The lilac form of Common White Inocybe (p.126) has brown gills.

Wood Blewit *Lepista nuda*

The large, thick-fleshed cap has a blue-violet tinge and incurved margin when young but older caps turn tan or grey from the centre and the margin becomes wavy. The sinuate, crowded gills fade from lilac to buff as does the solid, non-tapering stem. The smell is mild and fruity.

Size	Cap 5-15 cm, stem 5-10 cm x 15-25 mm.
Habitat	In leaf litter of woods, hedgerows and gardens.
Season	Autumn to late winter.
Edible	Must be well cooked. Watery when old.
Similar species	Field Blewit (p.28) lacks the lilac cap and gills. The smaller *L.sordida* has a brown cap and cyanide (bitter almond) smell. Violet species of Cortinarius (e.g. *purpurascens* p.122) have rusty-brown spores.

FIELD BLEWIT *Lepista saeva*

The large cap is initially convex with an inrolled edge, later flat or concave. It is pale, grey-brown, thick and fleshy. The grey-pink gills are sinuate and crowded. The short thick stem is streaked bright violet, especially near its base which is often swollen.

Size	Cap 5-12 cm, stem 4-10 cm x 15-25 mm.
Habitat	Grassland and woodland edges, often in rings.
Season	Autumn to early winter.
Edible	Stem and cap have firm flesh and a subtle taste. Dries well.
Similar species	Wood Blewit (p.27) has a violet cap and gills when young. *L.sordida* is pale violet-brown. St George's Mushroom (p.62) fruits earlier and lacks the lilac stem. Clouded Agaric (p.29) has a grey cap and decurrent gills.

CLOUDED AGARIC *Clitocybe nebularis*

A large fungus often growing in rings. The thick fleshy convex cap matures flat, often with a depressed centre and inrolled edge. It is grey-brown, darker at the centre and frequently with a white bloom. The gills are crowded, cream-coloured, adnate to slightly decurrent. The stem is paler, and thick with a swollen base. It smells strongly of turnip.

Size	Cap 8-20 cm, stem 5-12 cm x 20-30 mm.
Habitat	In litter of broad-leaved and coniferous woods.
Season	Autumn to early winter.
Edible	Can cause digestive upset so best avoided.
Similar species	It can be confused with Wood Blewit (p.27) which also has pale-pink spores and an inrolled cap edge but with sinuate, initially lilac-coloured gills and a fruity smell.

CLUB-FOOTED FUNNEL CAP *Clitocybe clavipes*

The cap has an inrolled edge, initially convex but later flat and often with a spongy central umbo. It is grey-brown to tan and the stem, which has a swollen base narrowing gently towards its apex, is paler. The gills are very decurrent, uncrowded and creamy-yellow. The smell is sweet and fruity.

Size Cap 4-8 cm, stem 4-7 cm x 10 mm (wider at base).

Habitat Coniferous or broad-leaved woods. Especially common in beech leaf litter.

Season Autumn.

Inedible Not worth eating and causes nausea and hot flushes when consumed with alcohol.

Similar species *C. geotropa* is paler and found on chalky soils. Other Funnel Caps lack the swollen stem base.

COMMON FUNNEL CAP *Clitocybe infundibuliformis*

Also known as *C. gibba*, its funnel-shaped, pale creamy-brown cap has a thin, wavy margin and very decurrent, crowded creamy-white gills. The smooth cream-coloured stem is tough and only slightly enlarged at its base. It smells of new-mown hay.

Size	Cap 4-8 cm, stem 3-7 cm x 6-10 mm.
Habitat	In leaf litter in broad-leaved woods and on heaths.
Season	Summer to autumn.
Edible	Not worthwhile.
Similar species	Often confused with Tawny Funnel Cap (*C. flaccida*) which grows in troops in woodland leaf litter. It has a larger red-brown cap, pale yellow gills and a woolly stem base.

ANISEED FUNNEL CAP *Clitocybe odora*

Easily identified by its strong aniseed smell and blue-green colour. The young blue-green cap is convex with an inrolled margin. Older flat caps dry to pale cream with a wavy margin. The adnate to slightly decurrent, green-tinged gills pale with age. The stem colour is similar to the cap's, the base with white down.

Size	Cap 3-6 cm, stem 4-8 cm x 5-10 mm.
Habitat	Woodland leaf litter, usually beech or oak.
Season	Late summer to autumn.
Edible	Thin-fleshed. Best dried.
Similar species	*C.fragrans* also smells of aniseed but has a smaller, yellow-brown cap, buff gills and a long thin stem. Verdigris Toadstool (p.118) is blue-green with brown gills and a ring on the scaly stem.

IVORY CLITOCYBE *Clitocybe dealbata*

One of the most poisonous of the small grassland fungi, it is a dirty-cream colour with pale ochre and flesh tones. Initially convex with an inrolled margin, the smooth cap becomes flat or slightly depressed and wavy-edged. The crowded, pale, flesh-coloured gills are shortly decurrent on to a creamy stem. It has a mealy smell.

Size	Cap 2-4 cm, stem 2-4 cm x 5-10 mm.
Habitat	Lawns and short grassland, often in rings.
Season	Midsummer to late autumn.
Poisonous	Excessive salivation and sweating shortly after ingestion. Can be fatal.
Similar species	The equally deadly *C.rivulosa* has a frosted cap surface and little or no smell. Fairy Ring Champignon (p.39) has widely spaced, adnexed gills.

33

WOOD WOOLLY-FOOT *Collybia peronata*

The dense woolly hairs at the stem base inspire the descriptive common name and cling to dead leaves. The thin leathery flat cap is red-brown to pale yellow as are the spaced, adnexed gills. The lower half of the slender stem is covered with yellow or pale brown woolly hairs.

Size	Cap 3-6 cm, stem 4-8 cm x 4-6 mm.
Habitat	Leaf litter of broad-leaved woods. Occasionally among coniferous needle litter.
Season	Late summer to autumn.
Inedible	It has a peppery taste. Sometimes used to add spice to certain dishes.
Similar species	Clustered Tough Shank (p.36) grows in tufts, has a finely hairy stem and more crowded gills.

RUSSET TOUGH SHANK *Collybia dryophila*

Living up to its name with a russet-brown, smooth hollow fibrous stem which is slightly swollen at the base. The thin flat dry cap is initially also russet but fades to pale buff. The very crowded, adnexed gills are creamy-white, sometimes pale yellow. Mushroom-like smell.

Size	Cap 2-5 cm, stem 3-6 cm x 2-4 mm.
Habitat	Gregarious among leaf litter in broad-leaved woods. Also under bracken on heaths.
Season	Midsummer to late autumn.
Inedible	Tough. Poisonous if eaten raw.
Similar species	The similar-coloured Spindle Shank (*C. fusipes*) has twisted, flattened stems swollen at the middle and fusing with others at the base. On or near oak and beech stumps.

CLUSTERED TOUGH SHANK *Collybia confluens*

Growing in dense clumps with thin stems attached at the base, the thin, flesh-brown convex caps mature flat and dry creamy-white. The slender pink-brown, frequently flattened hollow stem is usually darker than the cap and covered with tiny grey-white down. The gills are flesh-coloured, adnexed and crowded.

Size	Cap 2-5 cm, stem 6-10 cm x 3-5 mm.
Habitat	Among leaf litter in broad-leaved woods, mostly with beech and often in rings.
Season	Late summer to late autumn.
Inedible	Tough and not worth eating.
Similar species	Tufted Bell Cap (p.44) has more delicate, less flat caps and grows on oak stumps. Funnel Caps (pp. 30-32) grow in similar habitats but have decurrent gills.

GREASY TOUGH SHANK *Collybia butyracea*

This is fleshier than other common Tough Shanks and has a distinctive greasy or buttery feel, especially on the cap's umbo. This retains the date-brown colour which on most older caps dries pale buff. It has cream-coloured, crowded adnexed gills. The stem tapers from a much thicker base where it has fine white hairs.

Size	Cap 4-8 cm, stem 5-9 cm x 10 mm (average).
Habitat	Among broad-leaved tree litter and coniferous needle litter, often in troops and rings.
Season	Early autumn to early winter.
Edible	Not worthwhile.
Similar species	The uncommon *C.distorta* is red-brown, lacks the greasy feel and swollen stem base. Restricted to coniferous woods.

SPOTTED TOUGH SHANK *Collybia maculata*

This large, thick-fleshed, initially white species develops rusty-brown spots on its cap, gills and stem. Handling also causes browning. The deeply convex cap matures flat but often misshapen. The white gills are thin, adnexed and very crowded. The tall, broad, fibrous stem continues root-like underground.

Size	Cap 6-12 cm, stem 8-12 cm x 8-15 mm.
Habitat	Under trees, most commonly in coniferous woods. Also on heaths with bracken.
Season	Midsummer to late autumn.
Inedible	Very tough with a bitter taste.
Similar species	A similar-sized fungus which is also white with pinky-brown blemishes is *Tricholoma columbetta* but this has sinuate gills and smells of meal.

FAIRY RING CHAMPIGNON *Marasmius oreades*

This causes rings of dead grass in lawns. The small, tan, bell-shaped caps retain an umbo in old specimens which dry dirty-white. The wavy margins are often grooved when wet. The adnexed, cream gills are well spaced but have intermediates near the edge. The straw-coloured stem is tough and pliable. It smells of new-mown hay.

Size	Cap 2-5 cm, stem 3-6 cm x 2-4 mm.
Habitat	Among short grass in lawns.
Season	Early summer to late autumn.
Edible	Use dried in soups and stews. Beware confusion with poisonous species (see below).
Similar species	Often found growing with the poisonous Ivory Clitocybe (p.33) which lacks the grooved cap edge, has decurrent gills, a brittle stem and a mealy smell.

LITTLE WHEEL FUNGUS *Marasmius rotula*

This tiny, very beautiful fungus is tougher than it looks. The thin, creamy-white cap is radially furrowed like a parachute, from the darker, central depressed region to the scalloped margin. The cream, widely-spaced gills are attached not to the stem but to a collar round its apex, like the spokes from a wheel hub. The long red-brown, wiry stem is darker at the base.

Size	Cap 0.7-1.3 cm, stem 2-4 cm x 1-2 mm.
Habitat	On dead twigs, bark and occasionally leaf litter of broad-leaved trees.
Season	Midsummer to late autumn.
Inedible	It is tough and very small.
Similar species	Horse-hair Fungus (p.41) has a pinky-brown cap and more crowded gills attached to the stem. *M.epiphyllus* is white with a pale stem but no collar.

HORSE-HAIR FUNGUS *Marasmius androsaceus*

The dark-brown to black thin wiry stem is very like horse's hair. The convex cap is radially furrowed from a dark red-brown, slightly depressed central region; the rest is dull flesh-pink. The pinky-brown gills are adnately attached. The black stem is smooth, shiny and tough.

Size	Cap 0.5-1 cm, stem 3-5 cm x 1 mm.
Habitat	In large numbers on dead needles and twigs of coniferous species. Also on dead heather.
Season	Spring to early winter.
Inedible	Tough and insubstantial.
Similar species	*M.ramealis* is pinky-white with a much shorter, broader, often curved, scurfy stem. Most common on dead blackberry stems.

BONNET BELL CAP *Mycena galericulata*

The bell-shaped cap is light brown to grey, paler at
the margin which is furrowed and later upturned. It
flattens and wrinkles with age but retains a central
umbo. The gills are pale grey with a flesh tint,
adnate and spaced with cross veins. The stem is
smooth, often curved, the same colour as the cap,
with white hairs at its base. It smells of meal.

Size	Cap 2-6 cm, stem 3-8 cm x 2-5 mm.
Habitat	Clustered on broad-leaved stumps and fallen logs.
Season	Most of the year.
Edible	Insubstantial and not worth eating.
Similar species	Stump Bell Cap (p.43) is more densely tufted, has an ammonia-like smell and is associated with coniferous trees.

STUMP BELL CAP *Mycena alcalina*

A very common species, its Latin name comes from its alkaline, ammonia-like smell. The small, browny-grey, bell-shaped cap often has an olive tint. The margin is paler when wet, showing darker lines. The adnate gills ascend to the stem apex and are pale grey with a white margin. The thin smooth stem is cap-coloured.

Size	Cap 1-3 cm, stem 4-6 cm x 2 mm.
Habitat	In tufts on coniferous stumps; twigs and logs.
Season	Late summer to autumn.
Inedible	Not worth eating despite its mild taste.
Similar species	*M.leptocephala* has a comparable smell but is less robust, rarely clustered and occurs on woodland soil and among leaf or needle litter.

TUFTED BELL CAP *Mycena inclinata*

As its name suggests, this grows in tufts (on oak stumps). It is red-brown with a darker central umbo and a striate margin that extends beyond the white adnate gills which mature flesh-pink. The long, frequently twisted stem is off-white at the apex but more yellow-brown in the centre and dark red-brown at the base which is covered with white woolly hairs. It smells of rancid oil.

Size	Cap 2-3 cm, stem 4-10 cm x 2-3 mm.
Habitat	Densely tufted on oak stumps.
Season	Late summer to autumn.
Inedible	Not worth eating despite the mild taste.
Similar species	On stumps - Bonnet Bell Cap (p.42) lacks a dark stem base. *M.haematopus* has red-brown caps and stems which exude a red liquid when damaged.

44

MILKY BELL CAP *Mycena galopus*

The common name refers to the milky-white fluid which is exuded from the broken stems of young specimens. The conical cap has a brown central umbo, the remainder is paler and striated. (In var. *alba* the whole fruitbody is white.) It has adnate, ascending grey-white gills. The stem is grey, darker at the base. It smells faintly of radish.

Size	Cap 1-2 cm, stem 4-6 cm x 1-2 mm.
Habitat	Among leaf and needle litter of both broad-leaved and coniferous trees.
Season	Late summer to late autumn.
Edible	Not worth eating.
Similar species	The less common *M.leucogala* also exudes a white juice from its broken stem but the cap and stem apex is a deeper brown-black colour.

45

Small Bleeding Bell Cap Mycena sanguinolenta

The conical cap later flattens but maintains a dark red-brown central umbo. The rest is pinky-brown with darker striations. The adnate pinky-white gills have a red-brown margin. The hollow, long russet stem exudes a pink-red latex when broken.

Size	Cap 0.5-1.5 cm, stem 4-7 cm x 1 mm.
Habitat	Among moss in both broad-leaved and coniferous woods. Also on heaths.
Season	Summer to autumn.
Edible	Not worthwhile.
Similar species	The larger *M.haematopus* has a stem which exudes a darker red latex when damaged and grows clustered on rotting wood. The uncommon *M.crocata* occurs with beech litter and exudes an orange-red juice.

Lilac Bell Cap *Mycena pura*

It has quite a large cap (for a Bell Cap) and one which becomes flat or even slightly depressed around its central umbo. The margin is lined when moist. The cap and stem have a violet or purple hue. The adnate to almost decurrent, crowded gills are pale grey with a lilac tint and the stem is smooth and thick. It smells strongly of radish.

Size	Cap 2-5 cm, stem 3-8 cm x 3-8 mm.
Habitat	Among leaf litter in both broad-leaved and coniferous woodland.
Season	Summer to late autumn.
Poisonous	Contains muscarine.
Similar species	Some put the pink-coloured, non-umbonate form as a separate species - *M. rosea*. The edible Amethyst Deceiver (p.26) has spaced violet gills.

YELLOW-STEMMED BELL CAP _Mycena epipterygia_

The yellow stems of this species make it stand out despite its small size. The convex yellow-brown cap is semi-transparent with striations almost to its centre. Its smooth surface is slimy when moist. The white gills are adnate to slightly decurrent. The long slender stem is a bright lemon-yellow and sticky to the touch.

Size	Cap 1-2 cm, stem 4-8 cm x 1-3 mm.
Habitat	In coniferous woods among moss, grass and needle litter. Also on heaths.
Season	Late summer to autumn.
Edible	Too small to be worth eating.
Similar species	Other yellow-stemmed Bell Caps include _M. viscosa_ and _M. epipterygioides_. Both grow on wood, including stumps; the latter on conifers.

ORANGE BELL CAP Mycena acicula

This minute species is distinguished by its bright
orange colour. The tiny convex, orange cap is more
yellow at the striate, semi-transparent margin. The
pale yellow gills ascend to the top of the yellow,
thread-like stem which is whiter at the base.

Size	Cap 0.4-1 cm, stem 3-4 cm x 0.5-1 mm.
Habitat	Under conifers usually among moss.
Season	Summer to autumn.
Inedible	Insubstantial.
Similar species	The tiny *M.adonis* also grows in moss but has a pink cap and gills. The larger *M.flavoalba* is yellow with decurrent gills and grows in short grass. *M.acicula* is easily confused with Orange Moss Agaric (p.50) but this has very decurrent gills.

ORANGE MOSS AGARIC *Rickenella fibula*

This delicate white-spored fungus was previously included with the Mycenas from which it differs in having deeply decurrent gills. The convex cap flattens with age but has a centrally depressed region which is a darker orange. The margin is grooved and often wavy-edged. The pale orange, decurrent gills descend on to the yellow-orange stem which narrows to its base.

Size Cap 0.4-1 cm, stem 3-6 cm x 1 mm.
Habitat Among moss and short grass in damp places.
Season Summer to autumn.
Inedible Too small to be worth eating.
Similar The larger grey-brown *R.swartzii* (also known as
species *R.setipes*) grows in similar habitats. Orange Bell
Cap (p.49) has gills which ascend to the stem.

Umbrella Navel Cap *Omphalina ericetorum*

A common little fungus of moors and heaths, it is sometimes included in the genus *Gerronema*. The yellow-brown convex cap has a darker, centrally depressed area surrounded by a deeply grooved, inrolled margin – hence the name Navel Cap. Some of the widely-spaced, decurrent, pale ochre gills are forked. It has a smooth, pale brown stem.

Size	Cap 1-2 cm, stem 1-3 cm x 2-3 mm.
Habitat	On acid peaty soil among moss or lichens. Also on rotten wood.
Season	Early summer to late autumn.
Inedible	Insubstantial.
Similar species	*O.pyxidata* is red-brown with more crowded gills and grows on bare soil or in short grass. The darker *O.sphagnicola* grows on bog moss (*Sphagnum*).

○ ROOTING SHANK *Oudemansiella radicata*

The convex red-brown cap matures flat with a broad central umbo around which the surface is radially wrinkled. It is slimy when wet, shiny when dry. The white gills are broad and adnexed. The long, longitudinally grooved, tough stem is paler than the cap. It is darker and broader at the base before narrowing and continuing like a root.

Size	Cap 4-10 cm, stem 8-20 cm x 5-10 mm.
Habitat	On broad-leaved stumps or from roots and buried wood; mostly with beech. Singly or in small groups.
Season	Midsummer to autumn.
Edible	Not worth eating due to slimy cap.
Similar species	*O.longipes* (also known as *Xerula pudens*) has a dry, grey-brown, felty cap and a stem covered with red-brown velvety hairs.

PORCELAIN MUSHROOM *Oudemansiella mucida*

A beautiful fungus with a shiny, semi-transparent, porcelain-like appearance. The broadly convex, creamy-grey cap is wrinkled at the margin and very slimy when moist. It has broad, spaced, adnate cream-coloured gills. The stem is white above the large ring; the lower part is greyer, sticky and often bent to bring the cap to the horizontal.

Size	Cap 4-8 cm, stem 4-8 cm x 3-7 mm.
Habitat	Always on beech; stumps, fallen logs and also as a weak parasite on trunks and side branches of mature living trees. Usually clustered.
Season	Late summer to early winter.
Edible	The slime must be removed first.
Similar species	None.

VELVET SHANK *Flammulina velutipes*

This species continues fruiting through the winter. The medium-sized caps soon flatten and are a distinctive orange-brown, darker at the centre, slightly lined at the margin. The surface is shiny and sticky. The adnate, broad spaced white gills mature pale yellow. The stem is tough, velvety, cap-coloured at the apex and dark brown at the base.

Size	Cap 2-7 cm, stem 3-10 cm x 3-8 mm.
Habitat	Clustered on dead wood (stumps, logs and standing timber) of broad-leaved trees, typically on elm.
Season	Autumn to spring.
Edible	Remove the slimy layer and tough stem.
Similar species	Confusable with other tufted wood rotters such as Brown Stew Fungus (p.115) and Sulphur Tuft (p.116) but these have brown spores and a ringed stem.

HONEY FUNGUS *Armillaria mellea*

A destructive species, it kills a wide range of trees and shrubs and spreads to new hosts by bootlace-like strands. The deeply convex caps mature flat with an inrolled margin. The colour ranges from honey-yellow to red-brown. The gills are adnate to decurrent, crowded, flesh-coloured and later have rusty spots. The stem is long with a yellow-white ring; its brown base not swollen.

Size	Cap 5-15 cm, stem 6-12 cm x 10-20 mm.
Habitat	Densely clustered on both living trunks and dead stumps and roots of broad-leaved trees and conifers.
Season	Late summer to early winter.
Edible	Not easily digested. Must be well cooked.
Similar species	Bulbous Honey Fungus (see p. 56).

BULBOUS HONEY FUNGUS *Armillaria bulbosa*

Unlike Honey Fungus (p.55), this species does not kill trees, it simply rots dead wood. The cap is similar to Honey Fungus, with a more scaly top. The immature gills are covered with a cobweb-like veil that leaves a transient ring on the short, stocky stem which has a noticeably swollen base.

Size	Cap 5-15 cm, stem 4-10 cm x 20-30 mm.
Habitat	On tree stumps and dead wood mostly in small clumps and not densely clustered.
Season	Late autumn to early winter.
Edible	Not easily digested. Must be well cooked.
Similar species	Honey Fungus (p.55) lacks the bulbous base. *A.ostoyae* grows on conifers. Shaggy Pholiota (p.113) with brown spores has upturned brown scales on its cap and lower stem.

SOAP-SCENTED TRICHOLOMA *Tricholoma saponaceum*

The thick-fleshed, broadly convex cap has an incurved edge and ranges from olive to grey-brown but may be much paler at the margin. The smooth cap cracks when dry and is pink where damaged. It has broad, spaced, sinuate, cream to pale green gills. The cream stem often has grey-brown fibres or scales and is more pink below. It tapers to a root-like base.

Size   Cap 3-10 cm, stem 3-8 cm x 10-20 mm.
Habitat   In troops, usually under trees.
Season   Midsummer to autumn.
Inedible   Bitter taste. May cause digestive upset and easily confused with poisonous species.
Similar species   *T.ustale* has a sticky, chestnut-brown cap, no soapy smell and is found in broad-leaved woods.

GREY TRICHOLOMA *Tricholoma terreum*

The cap is initially bell-shaped and finally almost flat with a broad umbo. It is dark grey to black with radiating fibrils and an inrolled margin. The gills are broad, spaced, sinuate and grey-white. The stem is pale grey, smooth and cylindrical.

Size	Cap 4-8 cm, stem 3-7 cm x 10 mm.
Habitat	Most frequent under conifers.
Season	Late summer to autumn.
Edible	Has a mild taste but other grey Tricholomas are poisonous.
Similar species	*T.virgatum,* which grows on acid soils in coniferous woods, is of a similar size and also has grey-brown fibrils on the cap but the centre is markedly umbonate, the stem has a slightly swollen base and the flesh has a bitter, burning taste.

Scaly Tricholoma *Tricholoma argyraceum*

The cap is initially grey-brown and convex, maturing pale beige and flat but with scales at the centre and a wavy incurled margin which is covered with radiating fibres. It yellows from the margin when old or picked. The grey-white, broad sinuate gills also yellow with age. The stem is cylindrical and often bent. It smells faintly of flour. Also known as *T. sculpturatum*.

Size	Cap 3-7 cm x 3-6 cm x 5-10 mm.
Habitat	Under both broad-leaved (usually beech) and coniferous (usually pine) trees.
Season	Late summer to late autumn.
Edible	A mild taste but not very good eating.
Similar species	Grey Tricholoma (p.58) does not yellow and lacks both scales and smell.

YELLOW-BROWN TRICHOLOMA *Tricholoma fulvum*

The orange-brown cap flattens but for a broad, darker, central umbo and a faintly ribbed margin. The surface is smooth, shiny and sticky when young. The broad, sinuate yellow-brown gills often have darker spots. The stem apex is paler than the cap but darker at the stem base and covered with red-brown fibres. It is sticky when moist and has an unpleasant mealy smell.

Size	Cap 5-10 cm, stem 7-11 cm x 10-15 mm.
Habitat	On wet, acidic soils mostly under birch. Occasionally with conifers.
Season	Autumn.
Edible	Poor. Can be confused with other brown species.
Similar species	*T.ustale* with red-staining gills. *T.populinum* has white gills and grows under aspen and poplar.

SULPHUR TRICHOLOMA *Tricholoma sulphureum*

A number of woodland fungi have a yellow cap, stem and gills but this is the only one to smell strongly of coal-gas. The sulphur-yellow, matt cap surface often includes red-brown tints. It has similar-coloured broad, distant, sinuate gills. The yellow stem is covered with small brown fibrils.

Size	Cap 3-8 cm, stem 3-8 cm x 8-18 mm.
Habitat	Under broad-leaved trees e.g. oak or beech, more rarely under conifers.
Season	Autumn.
Inedible	The smell is unpleasant.
Similar species	*T.equestre* (previously *flavovirens*) is also yellow but has brown scales on its umbo. Yellow species of *Cortinarius* have adnate gills, brown spores and a cobweb veil when young (see p.121).

61

ST GEORGE'S MUSHROOM *Calocybe gambosa*

So called because it fruits as early as 23 April, though it is most frequent in May. The mealy smelling fleshy cap starts domed with inrolled edges but becomes flatter with wavy, often split margins. It is dry, smooth, creamy-white to pale tan. The white, sinuate gills are very crowded. The broad, solid, white stem is often curved and thicker at the base.

Size	Cap 5-12 cm, stem 4-10 cm x 20-40 mm.
Habitat	In pastures, road verges and lawns. Also among spring flowers in woodland edges and hedgerows.
Season	April to June.
Edible	Good when young; with a firm, dry flesh.
Similar species	Most similar-looking species fruit later but beware the poisonous Red-staining Inocybe (p.124).

CLUSTERED BROWN CAP *Lyophyllum decastes*

The fruitbodies are in crowded clusters. The almost hemispherical young caps age more convex with a broad central umbo where the grey to hazel-brown colour is darkest. The margin is wavy. The gills are adnate and a dirty white colour. The grey-white stem is usually flattened, bent and twisted, fusing with several others.

Size	Cap 6-10 cm, stem 5-10 cm x 10-18 mm.
Habitat	Near stumps or from buried wood in woodland, gardens, parks and even pavements.
Season	Midsummer to autumn.
Edible	Not highly rated. Beware highly poisonous lookalike Livid Entoloma (see p.107).
Similar species	*L.connatum*, is white with shortly decurrent gills. Beware the poisonous Livid Entoloma (p.107).

63

CHANGEABLE MELANOLEUCA *Melanoleuca melaleuca*

The smooth cap is dark brown when moist but dries much paler. The gills are crowded, white and weakly sinuate. The stem has pale brown fibres on a white background and is swollen at the base.

Size	Cap 4-10 cm, stem 4-8 cm x 10 mm.
Habitat	Among grass in pastureland and with leaf litter in woodlands. Solitary or in small troops.
Season	Late summer to autumn.
Edible	Insipid taste so not recommended.
Similar species	*M.cognata* is golden-brown with ochre gills and a mealy smell; it fruits in both spring and autumn in coniferous woods. Fawn Pluteus (p.101) is easily confused with *melaleuca* but has pink spores and always grows on rotting wood.

PLUMS AND CUSTARD *Tricholomopsis rutilans*

The name refers to the colour of the cap and gills. The large, flat cap is covered with fine red-purple scales, less dense near the incurved margins where the background yellow shows through. The apricot-yellow gills are weakly sinuate and crowded. The scaly, cap-coloured stem often curves. It has a musty smell.

Size	Cap 4-12 cm, stem 4-10 cm x 10-25 mm.
Habitat	On old conifer stumps, mostly with pine.
Season	Autumn.
Inedible	Not poisonous but not edible despite its name.
Similar species	The smaller, yellower *T.decora* also grows on conifer stumps.

IVORY WAX CAP *Hygrocybe nivea*

Also known as *Camarophyllus niveus*, its thin-fleshed cap is initially deeply convex but expands flat with an almost transparent, lined margin which often upturns to reveal the gill edges. It is smooth to greasy, pale beige when young and moist, but drying creamy-white. The gills are the same colour as the cap, broad, well-spaced and decurrent. The stem is cylindrical and white.

Size	Cap 2-5 cm, stem 2-5 cm x 4-8 mm.
Habitat	Among short grass in lawns, pastures and moors.
Season	Autumn to early winter.
Edible	Beware confusion with poisonous species.
Similar species	*H.virginea* is larger. The poisonous Ivory Clitocybe (p.33) has flesh-coloured gills. Fairy Ring Champignon (p.39) has adnexed gills.

YELLOW WAX CAP *Hygrocybe flavescens*

The pale orange to lemon cap has wavy, split margins which often reveal the gill edges. The smooth, shiny, slimy surface has lined margins when moist. The gills are pale yellow with a whiter edge, moderately crowded and deeply notched where they attach to the stem. The stem is drier, grooved and often flattened.

Size	Cap 3-6 cm, stem 5-7 cm x 5-10 mm.
Habitat	Among grass in lawns and short grass.
Season	Midsummer to autumn.
Inedible	Small and slimy, with an insipid taste.
Similar species	Other yellow Wax Caps include *H. chlorophana* with a slimy stem, the much smaller *H. vitellina* with decurrent gills, and the yellow and green Parrot Wax Cap (p.72).

67

ORANGE-RED WAX CAP Hygrocybe strangulata

The small, deep orange cap soon flattens with a paler, lined margin which is often split when old. The greasy cap surface later dries and the centre breaks up into small scales. The orange-yellow gills are adnate or shortly decurrent. The stem, similar in colour, is often flattened and tapers to a thinner, paler base. It is odourless.

Size	Cap 1-4 cm, stem 2-4 cm x 4-7 mm.
Habitat	In pasture and heathland on acid soil.
Season	Autumn.
Inedible	Not recorded as being worth eating.
Similar species	The larger, fleshier Meadow Wax Cap (p.70) is more tawny-apricot and the pointed Blackening Wax Cap (p.69) darkens with age. *H.ceracea* has a non-scaly cap and cross-veins between the gills.

BLACKENING WAX CAP *Hygrocybe nigrescens*

This striking species is one of several which blacken with age. The medium-sized, bell-shaped cap later becomes more convex. It is orange-red, slightly greasy and covered with small radiating fibrils. The wavy margin often splits. The broad, pale-yellow gills are almost free of the stem and have a toothed edge. The stem has a white base. The cap, gills and stem all blacken on handling and with age.

Size	Cap 4-7 cm, stem 4-10 cm x 5-10 mm.
Habitat	In grass on pastureland, lawns and road verges.
Season	Midsummer to autumn.
Inedible	Slightly bitter taste; edibility suspect.
Similar species	The slightly smaller *H.conica* has a more pointed, bright orange cap which also darkens with age. The rarer *H.calyptraeformis* has a conical lilac-pink cap.

MEADOW WAX CAP *Hygrocybe pratensis*

Also known as *Camarophyllus pratensis*, its convex cap becomes flat and concave but retains a broad, central umbo. The colour varies from apricot to tawny-buff and the greasy surface dries with age when the margin often splits. The thick, widely spaced waxy gills are decurrent and have cross-veins. The stout short stem narrows to its base.

Size	Cap 3-10 cm, stem 4-8 cm x 10-15 mm.
Habitat	Short grass of lawns, pastures and woods.
Season	Autumn to early winter.
Edible	Needs slow cooking. Mild taste.
Similar species	*H.quieta* is more orange and its gills are not decurrent. False Chanterelle (p.166) has an inrolled cap margin, crowded orange gills and a slender stem. Chanterelle (p.167) grows in moss in woods.

SCARLET HOOD *Hygrocybe coccinea*

The small bright cherry-red, convex cap is smooth and shiny when young and moist, but dries and fades to orange-pink with age. The thick orange-red gills pale with age. The attachment is adnate but with a small decurrent tooth. The cylindrical orange-red stem tapers to a pale base where it may become flattened.

Size	Cap 2-5 cm, stem 3-6 cm x 5-8 mm.
Habitat	Among short grass and moss in lawns and pasture.
Season	Late summer to early winter.
Edible	Not poisonous despite the orange-red flesh.
Similar species	The much larger and fleshier *H.punicea* has adnexed gills and dark-red cap flesh. The smaller, orange-red *H.miniata* has a dry cap, minutely scaly near the centre.

71

PARROT WAX CAP *Hygrocybe psittacina*

The bell-shaped cap has a lined margin and is very slimy. Older caps dry, flatten and lose their green colour, becoming yellow or even pink-tinged. The thick, adnate gills start green but age yellow from their margins. The slimy stem is initially green near the apex and yellow at the broader base but the green disappears with age. It is odourless.

Size	Cap 2-4 cm, stem 4-6 cm x 4-8 mm.
Habitat	Among grass in poor pasture and open woodland.
Season	Midsummer to late autumn.
Inedible	Not poisonous but not pleasant to eat.
Similar species	Older specimens are like the orange and yellow Wax Caps but these lack green tints. Verdigris Toadstool (p.118) is more blue-green and has almost black spores.

HERALD OF WINTER *Hygrophorus hypothejus*

Most fungi stop fruiting in late autumn but this occasional species does not appear until the frosts start, as its name suggests. Convex when young, flat later, the olive-brown slimy cap dries pale ochre. The margin remains inrolled until old. The broad, shortly decurrent, creamy gills mature pale orange. The young stem has a ring-like zone and is white and slimy; drying and ageing pale orange. It is odourless.

Size	Cap 3-5 cm, stem 5-7 cm x 5-10 mm.
Habitat	Among needle litter in coniferous or mixed woods, usually with pine.
Season	Late autumn to early winter.
Edible	Mild tasting but poor texture.
Similar species	*H.agathosmus* has a grey cap and cream gills.

COMMON YELLOW RUSSULA *Russula ochroleuca*

Russulas are unusual in that they can be readily crumbled. In this, the commonest of the yellow species, the convex cap soon flattens and may become concave. The matt, ochre-yellow, peelable skin matures with a faintly grooved edge. The pale cream gills are neat, adnate and quite crowded. The white cylindrical stem greys with age. The taste is acrid.

Size	Cap 4-10 cm, stem 4-8 cm x 10-20 mm.
Habitat	In both broad-leaved and coniferous woods.
Season	Late summer to early winter.
Edible	Peppery flesh is not to everyone's taste.
Similar species	Both Yellow-gilled Russula (p.75) and Geranium-scented Russula (p.77) have yellow gills. The bright yellow Yellow Swamp Russula (p.76) grows with birch in wet ground.

YELLOW-GILLED RUSSULA *Russula lutea*

This species is distinguished from the Common Yellow Russula (p.74) by its usually smaller, thin-fleshed, more convex cap which is golden or egg-yolk yellow. The brittle white stem is slightly broader at the base. The crowded adnate gills are a rich orange-yellow. Older specimens smell of apricots.

Size	Cap 2-6 cm, stem 2-6 cm x 6-12 mm.
Habitat	Under broad-leaved trees, especially oak.
Season	Late summer to autumn.
Edible	Mild tasting but rather insubstantial.
Similar species	The larger Geranium-scented Russula (p.77) has pale yellow gills and is distinguished by its darker cap, off-white stem, burning taste and geranium smell.

Yellow Swamp Russula *Russula claroflava*

Best identified by its habitat as it is confined to very wet ground under birch. The fleshy, bright yellow cap remains convex with a shiny, slightly sticky surface. The pale, ochre-yellow, adnexed gills are quite crowded. The stem is white and cylindrical. The gills and other parts bruise dark grey. It has a pleasant smell.

Size	Cap 4-10 cm, stem 5-10 cm x 10-20 mm.
Habitat	In wet ground under birch trees; often with *Sphagnum* (bog) moss.
Season	Summer to autumn.
Edible	Has a pleasant texture and taste.
Similar species	No other Russula has a clear yellow cap and such a specific habitat.

GERANIUM-SCENTED RUSSULA *Russula fellea*

This species is distinguished from Common Yellow Russula (p.74) which has a similar-coloured cap, by the fact that the yellow-brown cap colour is also found (slightly paler) on the gills and stem. The cap, initially sticky and convex, soon flattens and may become concave. It only peels at the margin, which is slightly furrowed. The gills are crowded, adnexed and straw-coloured like the cylindrical stem. It smells of geranium or cooked fruit.

Size	Cap 4-10 cm, stem 3-8 cm x 10-20 mm.
Habitat	Most frequent under beech trees.
Season	Autumn.
Inedible	The flesh has a very hot taste.
Similar species	The mild tasting, Yellow-gilled Russula (p.75) has a white stem.

STINKING RUSSULA *Russula foetans*

This large, honey-brown Russula has a slimy feel to its cap which is distinctly furrowed and warty at the margin which often matures wavy and split. The thick, spaced, adnate gills are dirty cream as is the hollow, frequently flattened stem. Both gills and stem age brown-spotted. It has an unpleasant oily smell, like rancid butter.

Size	Cap 6-15 cm, stem 6-15 cm x 20-40 mm.
Habitat	Under both broad-leaved and coniferous trees.
Season	Summer to autumn.
Inedible	Unpleasant smell and peppery cap flesh.
Similar species	The smaller *R.laurocerasi* has a similarly coloured, grooved cap but it is less sticky and smells of marzipan or bitter almonds.

FRAGILE RUSSULA *Russula fragilis*

While all Russulas are crumbly this small species is especially delicate, as its name implies. The thin-fleshed, flat cap is often depressed at the centre where it is a darker purple in contrast to the more violet or pink margin which is usually grooved. The pale cream adnate gills have toothed edges (visible only through a lens). The white stem is tinged with yellow and is swollen at the base. It smells of boiled sweets (pear drops).

Size	Cap 2-6 cm, stem 3-6 cm x 5-10 mm.
Habitat	Under both broad-leaved and coniferous trees.
Season	Late summer to autumn.
Inedible	Has a very acrid taste.
Similar species	Birch Russula (p.80) is more yellow-pink, has more distant white gills and lacks the fruity smell.

BIRCH RUSSULA *Russula betularum*

This small, thin-fleshed Russula is always found near birch. The convex to flat cap is pale red-pink with areas of yellow-buff. The furrowed margin is frequently warty. The entire skin can be peeled. The gills are adnexed, white and with a slightly toothed edge. The white stem is often longer than the cap diameter. The smell is faintly fruity.

Size	Cap 2-6 cm, stem 3-7 cm x 5-8 mm
Habitat	Under birch; often in moss on damp ground.
Season	Late summer to autumn.
Inedible	Very acrid taste.
Similar species	Other pink-red species are not restricted to birch and include Fragile Russula (p.79) and Bare-toothed Russula (p.81).

BARE-TOOTHED RUSSULA *Russula vesca*

Old specimens of this fungus are easily identified as the skin peels easily and pulls away from the cap margin revealing the tooth-like white flesh and gill tops. The cap colour varies from pinky-red to pale brown and often includes olive tints. The margin is shallowly furrowed. The adnexed, crowded, pale cream gills often fork near the stem and later discolour with rusty spots. The white, firm stem narrows at its base.

Size	Cap 5-10 cm, stem 4-10 cm x 10-25 mm.
Habitat	Broad-leaved woods, mostly with beech and oak.
Season	Midsummer to early autumn.
Edible	Pleasant nutty taste.
Similar species	*Russula nitida* has a similar-coloured, shiny cap with a peeling margin but pale yellow gills.

THE CHARCOAL BURNER *Russula cyanoxantha*

A very common species with a firm fleshy cap which is predominantly a mix of blue and yellow but often includes violet, grey, brown and green tints; like the many colours of a charcoal flame. The crowded white gills are adnexed, often forked and unusually pliable for a Russula. The solid white stem may show purple tints. The smell is indistinct. Charcoal Burner is much less crumbly than other Russulas.

Size	Cap 5-15 cm, stem 5-10 cm x 10-30 mm.
Habitat	Under broad-leaved trees, especially with beech.
Season	Summer to late autumn.
Edible	Mild taste and firm texture.
Similar species	*R.parazurea* has a grey-blue, scurfy cap and cream-coloured gills.

BLACKISH PURPLE RUSSULA *Russula atropurpurea*

This has the crumbly texture typical of a Russula but with a smooth, firm cap which starts convex but matures flatter with a central depression. A red-purple margin surrounds the dark purple to black centre and grey or brown patches. The gills are white, adnate and quite crowded. The white stem becomes streaked with grey and the base discolours pinky-brown. It smells faintly of apples.

Size Cap 4-12 cm, stem 3-6 cm x 10-20 mm.
Habitat Broad-leaved woodland, with beech and oak. Occasionally under conifers.
Season Summer to autumn.
Edible Must be cooked. Mild to slightly peppery.
Similar species Some forms of Crab-scented Russula (p.87) have a dark purple cap but the gills are straw-coloured.

83

BLACKENING RUSSULA *Russula nigricans*

This species varies considerably in shape, size and colour as it matures. The cap is initially small, dirty-white, deeply convex and with an inrolled margin; as it flattens it turns brown and finally large, concave and black. Cracks reveal the paler flesh below. The well-spaced adnate gills are very thick and start creamy-yellow but become spotted with red-brown and later turn black. The firm stem also darkens with age. It has a fruity smell.

Size	Cap 8-25 cm, stem 4-10 cm x 15-30 mm.
Habitat	All kinds of woodland but commonly with beech.
Season	Midsummer to early winter.
Edible	Good when young, later tough and full of maggots.
Similar species	*R.albonigra* has crowded, decurrent gills.

THE SICKENER *Russula emetica*

The best-known of the Russulas because of its reputation for causing sickness. The convex cap, which soon flattens, is thin-fleshed and easily broken. It is shiny and sticky when wet with easily peelable skin which is a brilliant cherry-red with some paler areas. The creamy-white adnexed gills are moderately spaced. The spongy white stem is swollen at the base. It has a slightly fruity smell.

Size Cap 5-10 cm, stem 4-8 cm x 15-20 mm.
Habitat Under conifers on moist acid soil, often with moss.
Season Midsummer to autumn.
Poisonous The acrid flesh causes vomiting.
Similar species Beechwood Sickener (p.86).

BEECHWOOD SICKENER *Russula mairei*

Unlike the Sickener (p.85), this species has a smaller, firmer, matt cap which is a lighter shade of scarlet and occasionally pink or almost white. The crowded white gills age slightly grey-green. The firm, solid stem yellows but does not swell at the base. It smells of coconut when young, sweeter when old.

Size	Cap 3-7 cm, stem 2-5 cm x 10-15 mm.
Habitat	Under beech trees.
Season	Autumn.
Poisonous	The acrid flesh causes sickness.
Similar species	The Sickener (p.85) has a larger, more fragile, deep red cap and grows under conifers. Other red Russulas are paler or have off-white gills or stems.

CRAB-SCENTED RUSSULA *Russula xerampelina*

As the picture shows this species can be found in a number of different-coloured varieties. The broadly convex smooth cap may be purple or brown or pale yellow or olive-green or a mixture of all. The thick adnexed gills are pale ochre and show cross veins at their bases. The white stem has a faint pink flush and browns towards its base and with handling. Old specimens smell strongly of crab.

Size	Cap 7-15 cm, stem 4-10 cm x 15-30 mm.
Habitat	In broad-leaved woods, mostly with beech and oak.
Season	Late summer to early winter.
Edible	Mild taste despite the crab-like smell.
Similar species	The smell of *xerampelina* distinguishes it from other common, similar-coloured Russulas.

87

GRASS-GREEN RUSSULA *Russula aeruginea*

The pale yellow-green cap has brown tints and a darker centre. The margin is usually grooved. The adnexed, crowded yellow-ochre gills sometimes fork. The white stem narrows at the base. It has no distinctive smell.

Size	Cap 5-10 cm, stem 5-8 cm x 8-15 mm.
Habitat	Most often found under birch trees.
Season	Summer to early autumn.
Poisonous	May cause digestive upset.
Similar species	Other green Russulas include *heterophylla* with crowded white, decurrent gills which fork near the stem; *virescens* (Green-cracking Russula) with a dry skin which cracks into a mosaic pattern; and green varieties of The Charcoal Burner (p.82) , normally dark green with shades of purple and bronze.

PEPPERY MILK CAP *Lactarius piperatus*

The woodland Milk Caps have a crumbly texture but differ from the Russulas (pp.74-88) in having decurrent gills which exude a latex (milk) when broken. Peppery Milk Cap has a medium, ivory-white, matt, funnel-shaped cap with an inrolled margin. The very crowded, cream-coloured, thin decurrent gills age pinky-yellow and exude an acrid milk when damaged. The stem is long and white.

Size	Cap 8-15 cm, stem 4-8 cm x 20-30 mm.
Habitat	Under broad-leaved trees.
Season	Late summer to late autumn.
Edible	Dried specimens have been used as a seasoning but the very acrid taste is not for the faint hearted.
Similar species	Fleecy Milk Cap (p.90) has a downy cap and thick, white gills which also exude a very hot milk.

FLEECY MILK CAP *Lactarius vellereus*

The convex cap soon flattens and the central depression gives it a shallow funnel-shape. The creamy-white surface is velvety especially near the inrolled margin. Older caps, up to the size of a dinner plate, have discoloured yellow or brown areas. The white, decurrent, distant gills exude lots of white milk when damaged. Older gills brown slightly. The stem is solid, white and stocky.

Size	Cap 10-25 cm, stem 4-10 cm x 20-40 mm.
Habitat	Broad-leaved woodland.
Season	Late summer to early winter.
Inedible	Acrid taste when young, poor texture.
Similar species	Peppery Milk Cap (p.89) has a long stem, smooth cap and crowded gills, *L.controversus* pink-buff cap patches and flesh-coloured gills.

OAK MILK CAP *Lactarius quietus*

A very common species always associated with oak. The broadly convex dry cap is centrally depressed when old and a dull red-brown colour with faint, concentric darker bands. The shortly decurrent creamy-brown, crowded gills age darker brown and exude a creamy-white milk. The slender stem is the same colour as the cap but darker near its base. It has a strange oily smell.

Size	Cap 4-9 cm, stem 4-10 cm x 6-12 mm.
Habitat	Only found in the vicinity of oak trees.
Season	Autumn.
Inedible	Slight bitter taste, unpleasant smell.
Similar species	Slimy Milk Cap (p.92) grows with beech. Small Brown Milk Cap (p.96) is smaller, lacks the cap zonation and is commonest under birch.

SLIMY MILK CAP *Lactarius blennius*

This species is commonly found in beech woods. The depressed cap is a strange mix of grey, olive and brown with concentric bands of darker spots. It is shiny and very slimy when moist. The shortly decurrent gills start cream but grey with age and on damage because the white milk dries grey. The stem is paler than the cap and slimy when young. There is no obvious smell.

Size	Cap 5-10 cm, stem 4-5 cm x 10-15 mm.
Habitat	Under broad-leaved trees, mostly with beech.
Season	Late summer to autumn.
Inedible	Slimy cap surface and very acrid taste.
Similar species	The much larger, slimy-capped, Ugly Milk Cap (p.93) is darker and typically grows under birch trees.

UGLY MILK CAP *Lactarius turpis*

Also called *L.plumbeus* due to its leaden colour, this large fungus has young convex caps which are olive-brown with a felty inrolled margin; the mature caps are dark-brown to black and flat or slightly depressed. It is sticky when moist. The shortly decurrent, creamy-buff, crowded gills are spotted with brown when old. They exude an abundant, acrid white milk. The stocky stem is the same colour as the cap, often with shallow pits.

Size   Cap 7-20 cm, stem 4-6 cm x 20-30 mm.
Habitat   Under birch, often among leaf litter or grass.
Season   Late summer to autumn.
Inedible   Not recommended due to its bitter taste.
Similar species   Slimy Milk Cap (p.92). Mostly with beech.

93

RUFOUS MILK CAP *Lactarius rufus*

The cap is deep red-brown, dry and slightly rough, flat or shallowly depressed but with a central pimple. The gills are shortly decurrent, crowded, pale creamy-yellow, ageing to the same colour as the stem which is similar to that of the cap but paler. Damaged gills exude a white milk.

Size	Cap 4-10 cm, stem 4-8 cm x 6-12 mm.
Habitat	Under conifers but also with birch.
Season	Summer to late autumn.
Inedible	The initially mild tasting milk becomes very acrid after about a minute.
Similar species	Curry-scented Milk Cap (*L.camphoratus*), similar in shape and colour but only half the size with watery white milk. *L.hepaticus* is dull red-brown with browny-red spotted gills and a white milk that dries yellow.

Sweet Milk Cap *Lactarius subdulcis*

Medium-sized, it is rich red-brown when young but paler with age. The depressed centre remains darker. The crowded gills are only shortly decurrent and mature from cream to pinky-buff. The slender stem is a similar colour to the cap near its base but much paler at its apex. Damaged gills release lots of white milk which does not dry yellow (test on a handkerchief).

Size	Cap 3-8 cm, stem 4-8 cm x 4-8 mm.
Habitat	Under broad-leaved trees, mostly with beech.
Season	Late summer to autumn.
Inedible	The milk initially tastes sweet but has a very bitter aftertaste.
Similar species	Small Brown Milk Cap (p.96) is more common under birch and has an orange-brown cap with a central pimple and white milk which dries yellow.

SMALL BROWN MILK CAP *Lactarius tabidus*

The orange-brown cap soon flattens but usually has a central pimple and is often wrinkled near the middle. The shortly decurrent, yellow-brown, crowded gills release only small amounts of white milk when damaged. This dries yellow on a handkerchief. The stem narrows from its darker-coloured base to the apex.

Size	Cap 2-4 cm, stem 2-5 cm x 4-8 mm.
Habitat	With broad-leaved trees and most common under birch in wet places, often among *Sphagnum* (bog) moss.
Season	Midsummer to autumn.
Inedible	Insubstantial with a slightly acrid taste.
Similar species	The darker Sweet Milk Cap (p.95) produces more plentiful milk which does not dry yellow.

COCONUT-SCENTED MILK CAP *Lactarius glyciosmus*

A small Milk Cap easily recognised by its coconut smell. The cap colour varies from grey-lilac to pinky-brown. It has a dry, downy texture, thin flesh and an incurled margin when young. The crowded decurrent gills are flesh-coloured and produce small amounts of white milk when damaged. The stem is paler than the cap, becoming hollow and fragile with age.

Size	Cap 2-5 cm, stem 3-6 cm x 4-8 mm.
Habitat	Under broad-leaved trees, mostly with birch.
Season	Late summer to late autumn.
Edible	Used for flavouring but has a fairly hot taste.
Similar species	The larger Grey Milk Cap (*L. vietus*) has a sticky cap and a milk which dries grey on the gills; these bruise pale brown.

WOOLLY MILK CAP *Lactarius torminosus*

This species causes griping pains if eaten without careful preparation. The cap is markedly funnel-shaped when fully grown, sticky at the centre when moist and with an inrolled margin which in young specimens has a texture of lambswool. The flesh-pink cap is marked with concentric, darker pink rings. The gills are pink, crowded and weakly decurrent. They exude a white milk. The pale pink solid stem matures hollow with some surface pits.

Size	Cap 6-12 cm, stem 6-10 cm x 10-20 mm.
Habitat	With birch on damp peaty soil.
Season	Late summer to autumn.
Poisonous	Parboiled it is eatable but not edible.
Similar species	*L.pubescens* has a paler, non-zoned cap. Saffron Milk Cap (p.99) has orange gills and milk.

SAFFRON MILK CAP *Lactarius deliciosus*

This beautiful fungus is infrequent in Britain. Its large funnel-shaped cap has an inrolled margin when young and is slightly sticky. It is cream to pinky-orange with concentric bands of deep orange and faint green patches when old. The bright orange gills are shortly decurrent, crowded and produce a carrot-coloured milk. The stocky hollow stem is marked on the surface with orange pits near its base.

Size	Cap 5-15 cm, stem 4-8 cm x 15-20 mm.
Habitat	Under pine trees.
Season	Late summer to autumn.
Edible	Best blanched before being fried.
Similar species	The commoner Spruce Milk Cap (p.100) has a smooth stem. *L.salmonicolor* has a less zoned cap.

SPRUCE MILK CAP *Lactarius deterrimus*

This species is frequently confused with Saffron Milk Cap (p.99) but is much commoner, especially in spruce plantations. The yellow-orange cap is zoned with darker rings and old specimens or those exposed to frost show considerable greening. The shortly decurrent pale orange gills release a bitter orange milk which turns wine-red and finally dark green. The stem is only rarely pitted at its base.

Size	Cap 5-12 cm, stem 3-7 cm x 10-15 mm.
Habitat	Under conifers; most often with spruce.
Season	Late summer to autumn.
Inedible	Cooking reduces the bitterness. Not recommended.
Similar species	Saffron Milk Cap (p.99) has orange pits at the stem base and a mild tasting orange milk.

FAWN PLUTEUS *Pluteus cervinus*

This species is an important wood rotter. The cap is mid to dark brown and smooth except for darker streaks, most prominent at the centre. The gills are free of the stem, crowded and initially white; later they take on a flesh-pink tinge as the pink spores mature. The solid, slender white stem is streaked with dark-brown fibres and swollen at the base. It has a faint radish smell.

Size	Cap 6-12 cm, stem 4-10 cm x 8-12 mm.
Habitat	On broad-leaved stumps, logs and sawdust.
Season	All year but most frequent in autumn.
Edible	Not highly rated due to its sharp taste.
Similar species	*Volvariella speciosa* also has free, pink gills but a creamy-brown cap. Stem emerges from a volva. Grows in rich grassland and on sawdust.

VEINED PLUTEUS *Pluteus umbrosus*

Although not as common as Fawn Pluteus (p.101) this beautiful fungus is frequent in the same habitat. The broadly convex sepia-brown cap is overlain with branching veins of dark brown, tiny velvety scales; especially near the centre. The crowded, free gills start white but mature pink with a dark brown edge. The pale brown stem has cap-like scales. It smells faintly of garlic.

Size	Cap 4-9 cm, stem 3-8 cm x 8-12 mm.
Habitat	On stumps and rotting wood of broad-leaved trees.
Season	Late summer to autumn.
Edible	Soft-fleshed and not highly recommended.
Similar species	Fawn Pluteus (p.101) lacks the vein-like velvety scales on its cap. *P.leoninus* has a smaller, smoother, bright yellow cap.

SILKY NOLANEA *Nolanea sericea*

This common species typifies the family with its pink gills and pink angular spores. It was previously called *Entoloma sericeum*. The convex cap expands flat with a central umbo. The young cap is moist, dark brown with a grooved margin, later fading from the centre to creamy-beige with a silky surface. The sinuate gills have a ragged edge and mature grey-pink; a pink spore print can be seen at the apex of the stem. It smells of meal.

Size	Cap 2-5 cm, stem 3-5 cm x 2-4 mm.
Habitat	On lawns and short grass; often in troops.
Season	Midsummer to autumn.
Inedible	Confusable with poisonous pink-spored species.
Similar species	The Miller (p.108) also smells of meal but has deeply decurrent, pale pink gills.

STRIATED NOLANEA *Nolanea staurospora*

Like the previous species, older caps become flat and fade to pale ochre but *staurospora* has a more fleshy, bell-shaped, russet-brown young cap, sticky when moist and markedly striated near its margin. It has crowded, adnexed, pale pink gills. The slender stem is striated with grey fibres and broadens at the base.

Size	Cap 3-5 cm, stem 4-8 cm x 3-6 mm.
Habitat	Poor pasture and grassy woods. Also on moorland.
Season	Midsummer to autumn.
Inedible	Too easily confused with poisonous species.
Similar species	The larger *Entoloma nidorosum* is found in damp places, often under willow. Pale brown cap has a striate margin and dries to a silky dirty-white. Distinctive smell like nitric acid or chlorine.

WHITE LEPTONIA *Leptonia sericella*

The young convex cap has a broad central umbo but matures funnel-shaped with a central depression. It is dry, creamy-white and slightly rough. The gills, quite spaced, are initially adnate and white but age decurrent and pink. Stem slender, white and shiny. It has a pleasant mushroomy smell. Also called *Alboleptonia sericella*.

Size	Cap 2-4 cm, stem 2-5 cm x 2-3 mm.
Habitat	Wet grassland and moorland.
Season	Late summer to autumn.
Inedible	Beware confusion with highly poisonous fungi.
Similar species	The Miller (p.108) has a mealy smell as does the very poisonous Ivory Clitocybe (p.33) but this has crowded, white gills and a white spore print. Ivory Wax Cap (p.66) has broad, distant gills.

BLUE LEPTONIA *Leptonia corvina*

There are a number of small, dark blue species with pink spores which were previously placed in the *Entoloma* genus. The photograph shows the blue-black colour (the French describe it as crow-like) of young convex caps and the paler, flat older caps which have a roughly fibrous margin. The adnate white gills mature pale pink. The slender stem has a white base.

Size	Cap 1-3 cm, stem 2-6 cm x 2-3 mm.
Habitat	In short grass, especially amongst moss.
Season	Summer to autumn.
Poisonous	Some blue Leptonias are poisonous, so avoid.
Similar species	*L.serrulata* has grey-pink gills with a distinctive black edge and is more common in upland pasture. *L.lampropus* has a grey-brown cap and blue stem.

LIVID ENTOLOMA *Entoloma lividum*

Also known as *Entoloma sinuatum*, it has been mistaken for various edible fungi. The medium-sized, fleshy cap has a broad central umbo and a wavy, inrolled edge. The matt surface dries smooth and shiny. The colour varies from creamy-white through dirty-yellow to grey-brown. The sinuate gills age from straw-yellow to salmon-pink. The stem is stout and fibrous at the base. It has a mealy smell when young which later becomes more rancid.

Size	Cap 6-18 cm, stem 5-10 cm x 15-20 mm.
Habitat	Field edges, open woodland on rich soil.
Season	Summer to autumn.
Poisonous	Causes gastric upset and liver damage.
Similar species	St George's Mushroom (p.62) has a similar size, shape and smell but has white gills and spores.

THE MILLER *Clitopilus prunulus*

The young creamy-white convex cap has an inrolled edge. Later it is funnel-shaped with a wavy edge. The deeply decurrent white gills mature pink. The short white stem is often not central. It has a strong mealy smell and feels like kid leather.

Size	Cap 4-10 cm, stem 3-4 cm x 6-12 mm.
Habitat	Among grass including parkland and woodland.
Season	Late summer to autumn.
Edible	Excellent; the firm flesh tastes of meal. Beware confusion with poisonous species (see below).
Similar species	The poisonous Ivory Clitocybe (p.33), though smaller, has a similar shape and habitat. Cap surface is glossy, the spores white and the weakly decurrent gills are white, not pink.

APRICOT FUNGUS *Rhodotus palmatus*

This once rare species is now much commoner thanks to Dutch Elm disease providing large quantities of dead elm on which *Rhodotus* grows. The broadly convex cap is wrinkled and gelatinous. It starts deep pink with an inrolled edge but matures flatter and apricot-coloured. The sinuate, crowded gills are paler than the cap and have cross-connecting veins. The pale pink stem is often curved. It smells of apricots.

Size	Cap 5-10 cm, stem 3-6 cm x 8-12 mm.
Habitat	On stumps and fallen dead wood; mostly on elm.
Season	Early autumn to winter.
Inedible	The flesh has a very bitter taste.
Similar species	Not easily confused with other species.

EGG YOLK FUNGUS *Bolbitius vitellinus*

A thin-fleshed, fragile little species, also known as the Cow-pat Toadstool. The young cap is distinctly conical and the centre is shiny, slimy and egg-yolk yellow; the margin paler and grooved. Older caps are flat, pale ochre-brown with a translucent edge. The straw-coloured gills mature rusty-brown. The delicate pale yellow stem is more slender when growing in long grass.

Size	Cap 1-3 cm, stem 5-10 cm x 2-4 mm.
Habitat	Often solitary; on dung, rotting hay or straw, compost and well-manured grassland.
Season	Late summer to autumn.
Inedible	Insubstantial and with a slimy texture.
Similar species	Fairy Parasol (p.143) has black spores.

BROWN BELL CAP *Conocybe tenera*

Common in short grass where it is frequently confused with other small brown-capped species. The orange to ochre-brown cap remains bell-shaped with a striate margin when moist but dries yellowy-cream. The crowded brown gills ascend to the stem apex. The delicate pale ochre stem has a powdered surface.

Size	Cap 1-3 cm, stem 4-8 cm x 2-4 mm.
Habitat	Among grass in lawns, pasture and open woodland.
Season	Late spring to late autumn.
Inedible	Insubstantial.
Similar species	Some related *Conocybe* species are not easily distinguished. Magic Mushroom (p.120) has a pointed cap and almost black gills. Dung Roundhead (p.119) has a rounded cap and dark brown gills.

SPRING AGARIC *Agrocybe praecox*

The small to medium-sized cap is broadly convex and a pale tan colour which soon fades to creamy-beige. A cream-coloured veil protects the gills on young specimens and then leaves remains at the cap margin and as a ring at the stem apex on older ones. The adnexed, crowded, cream-coloured gills mature dingy-brown. The stem is paler that the cap and has a bulbous base.

Size	Cap 3-6 cm, stem 7-9 cm x 6-12 mm.
Habitat	In grass often in open woods and under hedges.
Season	Spring to summer. Occasionally in autumn.
Edible	Must be well cooked; not recommended.
Similar species	Can be confused with Field Mushroom (p.132). which has a fleshier cap and free gills which start pink but age very dark brown.

SHAGGY PHOLIOTA *Pholiota squarrosa*

The broadly convex, yellow-ochre cap is covered in concentric rings of upturned, triangular, red-brown scales. The margin remains inrolled. The crowded, straw-coloured adnate gills mature rusty-brown. The long, often curved stem narrows at its base. Below the scruffy ring are cap-like scales; above it is paler and smooth. It has a sharp radish-like smell.

Size	Cap 4-12 cm, stem 6-15 cm x 7-15 mm.
Habitat	In clusters on stumps or standing dead wood of broad-leaved trees, especially beech and rowan.
Season	Summer to autumn.
Inedible	The bitter flesh is difficult to digest.
Similar species	*P.flammans* is yellower as is the smooth *P.alnicola* (on alder and birch).

CHARCOAL PHOLIOTA *Pholiota highlandensis*

A small fungus frequently found on old bonfire sites hence its common name and the former Latin name, *P. carbonaria*. It has an orange-brown cap, shiny and slightly sticky with a paler, often wavy margin. The crowded, adnate gills are clay-brown with an olive tint. The stem is paler than the cap at the apex but darker near the base where it is covered in tiny red-brown scales. The ring zone soon disappears. It has no distinctive smell.

Size	Cap 2-6 cm, stem 3-6 cm x 4-8 mm.
Habitat	In troops on charred wood and burnt ground.
Season	Autumn to early winter.
Inedible	Insubstantial.
Similar species	The specific habitat of Charcoal Pholiota distinguishes it from related species.

BROWN STEW FUNGUS *Kuehneromyces mutabilis*

Brown and shiny when moist, the cap dries pale tan - hence '*mutabilis*' and the alternative common name, Two-toned Pholiota. The crowded, adnexed gills darken from cream to russet-brown. The slender, often curved stem is pale tan and smooth above the ragged ring (which often disappears) but dark brown from the small scales nearer its base.

Size	Cap 3-8 cm, stem 3-8 cm x 4-8 mm.
Habitat	In tufts on broad-leaved stumps and logs.
Season	Spring to winter.
Edible	The caps add flavour and colour to stews.
Similar species	The poisonous *Galerina marginata* grows singly on dead conifer wood. See also Velvet Shank (p.54) and Sulphur Tuft (p.116).

Sulphur Tuft *Hypholoma fasiculare*

The young caps are bell-shaped, smooth and rich sulphur-yellow, with gills covered by a pale, cobweb-like veil. They are later convex with a tan centre and pale yellow margin, often bearing veil remnants, now darkened by the spores. The gills are crowded, initially yellow but later olive-green to black from the spores. The slender stem curves at its base. There is a purple-brown ring zone.

Size	Cap 2-6 cm, stem 5-12 cm x 5-10 mm.
Habitat	In tufts on stumps and dead wood of broad-leaved trees; also on conifers.
Season	Throughout the year.
Poisonous	Very bitter with a taste like quinine.
Similar species	Brick Caps (p.117) are darker. Velvet Shank (p.54), has a slimy cap and a velvet stem.

BRICK CAPS _Hypholoma sublateritium_

Similar to the previous species but with fewer in a
tuft. The fleshy caps are brick-red near the centre
and pale tan at the margin which typically bears
white veil remnants. The creamy-yellow adnate gills
mature grey-brown. The stem is yellow above the
dark brown ring zone, increasingly red-brown below.

Size	Cap 4-8 cm, stem 6-10 cm x 8-12 mm.
Habitat	On tree stumps, dead wood and dead roots.
Season	Autumn.
Inedible	Less bitter than Sulphur Tuft but not edible.
Similar species	The much less common _H.capnoides_ has a slightly sticky, tan-coloured cap and grey gills when young. It grows on conifer stumps. Mild-tasting and edible but do not mistake for Sulphur Tuft (p.116).

VERDIGRIS TOADSTOOL *Stropharia aeruginosa*

Fresh specimens have slimy, shiny caps; young ones are dark, blue-green and bell-shaped, older ones more convex and grass-green. The cap margin is peppered with small white scales. Old caps lack slime and scales, fading to pale tan. The crowded, sinuate gills start pale grey but age purple-brown with a white margin. The stem is white above the transient ring (coloured by the purple-black spores); it is pale blue-green with white scales below (as cap margin).

Size	Cap 2-6 cm, stem 4-8 cm x 5-10 mm.
Habitat	Among grass in woods and in pasture.
Season	Midsummer to autumn.
Poisonous	Fortunately the colour is offputting.
Similar species	Specimens with smooth cap and stem are sometimes placed under *S.caerulea*.

DUNG ROUNDHEAD *Stropharia semiglobata*

A very common small brown fungus with an unusual shape likened to half a marble on a match stick. The hemispherical, ochre cap rarely flattens and is slimy when moist, sticky when dry. The adnate crowded gills do not ascend before joining the stem. The young pale grey gills age dark brown. The pale yellow, slender stem is sticky below a transient ring.

Size	Cap 1-3 cm, stem 4-10 cm x 2-3 mm.
Habitat	In and by dung in pasture and on manured soil.
Season	Late spring to late autumn.
Inedible	Insubstantial and slimy-textured.
Similar species	Dung-loving species of *Panaeolus* (pp.146 & 147) have bell-shaped caps and mottled brown gills. Magic Mushroom (p.120) has a pointed cap, ascending gills and a wavy stem.

MAGIC MUSHROOM *Psilocybe semilanceata*

Previously known as Liberty Cap, the new name came in during the 1960s along with its notoriety as a hallucinogen. The bell-shaped cap usually narrows to a point. Slimy and date-brown when moist, it dries pale straw, often with a furrowed margin. The crowded gills ascend to the stem apex. Initially grey, they mature almost black with a white edge. The slender wavy stem blues at the base.

Size	Cap 0.5-1.5 cm, stem 2-5 cm x 2-3 mm.
Habitat	In grass (lawns, playing fields, pastures.)
Season	Summer to autumn.
Poisonous	Affects sensory perception. Unpleasant taste.
Similar species	*P.coprophila* and *P.merdaria* grow on dung. Brown Bell Cap (p.111) has ochre-brown caps and gills. See also *Panaeolus* (pp.146 & 147).

RED-BANDED CORTINARIUS *Cortinarius armillatus*

There are hundreds of species of Cortinarius. One of the more frequent, C. *armillatus* has a rust-coloured, fleshy cap with slightly darker fibres near the centre and red-brown veil remnants at the margin. It has adnate rusty-brown gills. The chunky, pale tan stem is encircled by one or more orange-red bands and is swollen at its base.

Size	Cap 6-12 cm, stem 6-15 cm x 10-20 mm.
Habitat	Mostly with birch on acid heathland.
Season	Autumn.
Inedible	Some species are very poisonous.
Similar species	C. *speciosissimus* has a smaller cap and yellow veil remnants on a tawny stem. With conifers.

PURPLE CORTINARIUS *Cortinarius purpurascens*

The cap is broadly convex, wavy-edged and a mix of grey-brown and violet. There is a purple hue to the cortina. The young adnexed, purple gills brown with age as the spores develop. The broad cap-coloured stem has a swollen base and bruises violet. The flesh is purple with a fruity smell.

Size	Cap 5-12 cm, stem 6-12 cm x 15-25 mm.
Habitat	Under broad-leaved and coniferous trees.
Season	Autumn.
Inedible	Reported to produce digestive upset, so avoid.
Similar species	*C. violaceus* has a dark violet cap, gills and stem. The pale brown *C. largus* has blue tints on the cap and gills. *C. pseudosalor* has a sticky brown cap, violet-edged brown gills and violet stem base.

BLOOD-RED CORTINARIUS *Cortinarius sanguineus*

Allso known as *Dermocybe sanguinea*, it grows under conifers unlike the very similar C. *puniceus* shown in the photograph which grows with broad-leaved trees. The cap is covered in silky fibres. The red gills darken as the rusty-brown spores mature. The stem base is covered in a pale down.

Size Cap 2-5 cm, stem 3-6 cm x 3-8 mm.

Habitat *sanguineus* conifers; *puniceus* broad-leaved trees.

Season Autumn.

Poisonous Confusable with the very poisonous C. *orellanus*.

Similar species C. *semisanguineus* has red gills but a yellow-brown cap and stem. C. *cinnabarinus* (under beech) has all parts orange-red. C. *orellanus* is orange-yellow.

RED-STAINING INOCYBE *Inocybe patouillardii*

I.patouillardii is one of the largest woodland Inocybes with a fleshy, silky, conical cap. Typically cream to straw-coloured, it ages brick-red on the radiating fibres and when bruised. The crowded, adnexed gills start pale pink but age olive-yellow and bruise brick-red as does the stout white stem. The smell is fruity, later becoming foetid and unpleasant.

Size	Cap 3-8 cm, stem 3-10 cm x 10-15 mm.
Habitat	In grass at woodland edges; mostly on chalk.
Season	Late spring to autumn.
Poisonous	Causes death by heart failure or asphyxiation.
Similar species	The edible St George's Mushroom (p.62) has white gills, does not stain red and smells of meal.

STRAW-COLOURED INOCYBE *Inocybe fastigiata*

Its conical cap often splits at the margin when expanded but retains a raised, pale brown central area. The rest of the cap is straw-yellow and covered with grey-brown, radiating fibres. The gills are crowded and olive-brown. The slim, pale stem is not swollen at its base. Also known as *Inocybe rimosa*.

Size Cap 3-7 cm, stem 5-8 cm x 5-10 mm.

Habitat Broad-leaved woods especially with beech.

Season Midsummer to autumn.

Poisonous Dangerous due to its muscarine content.

Similar species *I. maculata* has darker brown fibrils and white down at the cap centre. *I. asterospora* also has brown fibrils but a fawn-coloured stem with a very swollen base.

COMMON WHITE INOCYBE *Inocybe geophylla*

This little fungus occurs in both a white form and with a lilac cap and stem in var. *lilacina* (Lilac Inocybe). The conical cap flattens but keeps a central umbo. The adnate, crowded gills mature from cream to dirty-brown. The thin stem is covered with silky fibres.

Size	Cap 1-4 cm, stem 2-5 cm x 3-4 mm.
Habitat	Gregarious, often by paths in woods.
Season	Summer to autumn.
Poisonous	Dangerous as it is easily confused with edibles.
Similar species	Both forms look like Bell Caps (pp. 42-49) which have white spores. Lilac Inocybe is confused with Amethyst Deceiver (p.26) but this has distant purple gills and white spores. *I. griseolilacina* is paler lilac and has small brown scales at the cap centre.

POISON PIE *Hebeloma crustuliniforme*

A common brown fungus which beginners find difficult to identify. The convex, pale tan, smooth cap is sticky when moist, with an inrolled margin. The sinuate grey-brown gills have a pale margin which exudes drops of water (not easily seen). The apex of the tan stem is covered with mealy white scales which rub off with handling. Sharp smell of radish or freshly cut potato.

Size	Cap 4-10 cm, stem 4-7 cm x 5-10 mm.
Habitat	Under broad-leaved trees, often in rings.
Season	Early autumn to early winter.
Poisonous	Very bitter, causing gastric upset.
Similar species	The smaller *H. anthracophilum* is darker, has a pliable stem and grows on burnt ground. *H.sinapizans* has a larger dry cap and a swollen stem base.

DARK-CENTRED HEBELOMA *Hebeloma mesophaeum*

Also known as Pine Mesophaeum, it grows under conifers and broad-leaved trees. The broadly convex cap is slimy and a rich chestnut-brown at the centre, pale creamy-brown at the margin. The crowded pinky-brown, sinuate gills are protected by a cobweb-like veil when young. The white stem sometimes has a faint brown ring zone (veil remnants) about halfway up and widens to a brown base. It has a faint smell of radish.

Size	Cap 2-5 cm, stem 4-7 cm x 5-12 mm.
Habitat	Under conifers and other trees especially birch.
Season	Late summer to autumn.
Inedible	Avoid as related species are poisonous.
Similar species	*H. pusillum* has a similar cap colour but clay-brown gills. Under willows.

RUSTY WOOD ROTTER *Gymnopilus penetrans*

This attractive fungus is rusty or tawny-brown on its cap, gills and stem. The medium-sized, bell-shaped cap soon flattens but often has a wavy margin. It is thin-fleshed and with a dry silky feel. The crowded pale-yellow, adnate to weakly decurrent gills darken with age and discolour with rust-coloured spots. The golden stem is darker below its middle and has a white, woolly base. Young stems bear a fibrillose ring.

Size	Cap 4-8 cm, stem 4-7 cm x 5-8 mm.
Habitat	Conifer stumps, logs and chippings.
Season	Late summer to autumn.
Inedible	Tough and with bitter-tasting flesh.
Similar species	Spectacular Gymnopile (p.130) is much larger. In tufts on dead wood of broad-leaved trees.

129

SPECTACULAR GYMNOPILE *Gymnopilus junonius*

Previously known as *Pholiota spectabilis*, its large, dry, fleshy convex cap retains a broad umbo after expanding. A vivid golden-orange, it is covered by tiny flattened, similar-coloured, fibrous scales. The adnate yellow gills age rusty-orange. The thick stem is often broader in the lower region before narrowing to a root-like base. Young specimens have a shaggy ring covered with rusty spores.

Size	Cap 6-15 cm, stem 6-18 cm x 15-30 mm.
Habitat	In clusters from the base of broad-leaved trees. Also on stumps and rotting logs.
Season	Summer to early winter.
Inedible	Bitter. Wrongly recorded as hallucinogenic.
Similar species	*Pholiota alnicola* is smooth and yellow.

MOSS PIXY CAP *Galerina vittiformis*

Moss Pixy Cap has a bell-shaped shiny, russet-brown cap, with a ribbed margin. The adnate gills are rust-coloured with a white edge. The slim tan stem is browner near the base and covered with a bloom near the apex.

Size	Cap 1-2 cm, stem 3-6 cm x 1-2 mm.
Habitat	Among moss in woods, heaths and grassland.
Season	Spring to autumn.
Inedible	Too small to be worth eating.
Similar species	Also growing in moss, *G. hypnorum* has a honey-brown cap and a mealy smell. *G. paludosa* .is dull-brown and odourless. Orange Moss Agaric (p.50) has decurrent white gills and white spores.

FIELD MUSHROOM *Agaricus campestris*

This is the best-known of about 40 species of *Agaricus*. The young (button) white cap is firm, smooth and domed. It expands flat and the centre may bear small, pale brown scales and the initially inrolled margin, untidy veil remnants. The young gills are protected by a white veil; they are crowded and free. They change from deep pink through brown to black. There is a transient ring on the stocky white stem. It has a pleasant smell.

Size	Cap 3-10 cm, stem 3-7 cm x 10-15 mm.
Habitat	Short grass in lawns, parks and pasture.
Season	Early summer to late autumn; following rain.
Edible	Excellent. Can be eaten raw but see below.
Similar species	Yellow Staining Mushroom (p.135) is poisonous to some; it has an unpleasant smell.

CULTIVATED MUSHROOM *Agaricus bisporus*

The shop mushroom is uncommon out of cultivation but too well-known to ignore. It is very similar to Field Mushroom (p.132) but the mature caps are typically darker due to a covering of brown, fibre-like scales. The crowded free gills are pink in young specimens; very dark brown in old flat caps. The stem bears a more permanent, large white, shaggy ring. Unlike Field Mushroom, the cut flesh reddens slightly.

Size	Cap 3-10 cm, stem 3-6 cm x 10-15 mm.
Habitat	In rich soil, dung heaps and mushroom compost.
Season	Summer to autumn.
Edible	Can be eaten raw. Older ones have more flavour.
Similar species	The brown-capped variety is similar to some of the Wood Mushrooms (p.136).

HORSE MUSHROOM *Agaricus arvensis*

A large fleshy species smelling of aniseed or bitter almonds. The deeply domed young white cap matures flat. Mostly smooth but may break up into scales at the margin. Older caps have an ochre tinge and flush dull yellow-ochre when bruised. The free grey gills mature dark-brown. The white stem also bruises yellow-ochre. The swollen base does not yellow when cut. It has a large two-layered ring, the lower part star-shaped.

Size	Cap 5-20 cm, stem 5-15 cm x 15-20 mm.
Habitat	Permanent pastures and road verges; often in rings.
Season	Early summer to late autumn.
Edible	Excellent flavour and texture but see below.
Similar species	See the poisonous Yellow Staining Mushroom (p.135).

YELLOW-STAINING MUSHROOM *Agaricus xanthodermus*

This species causes sickness and diarrhoea in a substantial minority. The button stage is unusual in that it is flat-topped. The white cap is minutely scaly at the centre and on bruising rapidly turns bright yellow, especially near the margin. The young white gills turn grey-pink and finally dark brown. The white stem bears a large, down-turned ring and a swollen base; the cut flesh of which turns chrome-yellow. It has an unpleasant smell, like ink or stale urine.

Size Cap 5-10 cm, stem 6-10 cm x 10-18 mm.
Habitat In grassland, gardens, hedgerows and woods.
Season Summer to autumn.
Poisonous Many are unaffected but best avoided.
Similar species *A. silvicola* (Wood Mushroom) stains yellow but not in the cut stem.

BLEEDING BROWN MUSHROOM *Agaricus haemorrhoidarius*

The hazel-brown cap surface breaks into small fibrous scales. The pale pink, free gills age darker and bruise red on handling. The tall, hollow white stem is minutely scaly below the large floppy brown ring and bruises dark red. The cut flesh in the stem and cap also reddens. It has a faint mushroomy smell.

Size   Cap 8-12 cm, stem 8-10 cm x 15-20 mm.

Habitat   In leaf litter of broad-leaved woods.

Season   Autumn.

Edible   Good to eat despite the 'bleeding flesh'.

Similar species   Brown Wood Mushroom (*A. silvaticus*) grows under conifers. The stem and large scaly cap of The Prince (*A. augustus*) stain yellow on bruising; the flesh does not redden and smells of almonds. Edible.

SHAGGY INK CAP *Coprinus comatus*

Young specimens show little stem beneath the finger-shaped, smooth white caps which become rugby-ball shaped with a smooth, dirty-brown apex; the rest breaks up into white or pale brown shaggy scales. The cap base expands and dissolves into an inky fluid, resulting in a small flat cap on a long stem. The crowded, free gills hang down and change from white through pink to black. The smooth, white hollow stem has a transient ring.

Size Cap 5-15 cm, stem 8-30 cm x 10-15 mm.
Habitat Grass, woodland vegetation and urban sites.
Season Spring to early winter.
Edible Must be eaten young. Good salty flavour.
Similar See Common Ink Cap (p.138) and Magpie Ink
species Cap (p.139).

COMMON INK CAP *Coprinus atramentarius*

The grey to fawn cap is initially egg-shaped, later bell-shaped. The smooth surface breaks into a few tiny scales at the apex; the margin is often wavy and split. The ascending gills mature from white to grey and finally black when they dissolve into an inky fluid. It has a smooth, hollow white stem with an ill-defined ring zone.

Size	Cap 4-8 cm, stem 5-15 cm x 10-15 mm.
Habitat	Gregarious from tree stumps or in grass, gardens, pavements - wherever buried wood is present.
Season	Spring to early winter.
Poisonous	It reacts with alcohol in the bloodstream causing nausea and hot flushes.
Similar species	The woodland *C. acuminatus* is smaller.

MAGPIE INK CAP *Coprinus picaceus*

The young, finger-shaped white cap is similar to that of Shaggy Ink Cap (p.137) but as the stem lengthens the cap becomes more bell-shaped and the white breaks into patches on a dark brown background. The pale pink ascending gills turn black and dissolve into an ink-like fluid. The white stem has a slightly frosted surface and lacks a ring. It smells of tar.

Size	Cap 6-10 cm, stem 10-20 cm x 15-20 mm.
Habitat	Under broad-leaved trees, mostly with beech.
Season	Autumn.
Inedible	Unpleasant smell. Possibly poisonous.
Similar species	The much smaller, more common *C. cinereus* grows on dung and manure. White scales mostly confined to the apex of the grey-black, conical cap.

RUSTY CARPET INK CAP *Coprinus domesticus*

Beginners often confuse this with Glistening Ink Cap (p.141) but the shaggy, rust-coloured vegetative strands at the stem base help to separate them. The bell-shaped, tan-coloured cap has a rusty-brown apex dusted with white granular scales and a grooved margin. The crowded white gills age dark grey with a purple tint before dissolving. The smooth white stem has a swollen base.

Size	Cap 2-5 cm, stem 4-8 cm x 4-5 mm.
Habitat	On dead wood and stumps of broad-leaved trees.
Season	Early summer to early autumn.
Inedible	Not worth eating.
Similar species	The less common *C. xanthothrix* also grows from a rust-coloured mat but has pale brown cap scales. Glistening Ink Cap (p.141) lacks the rust mat.

GLISTENING INK CAP *Coprinus micaceus*

More easily identified from young specimens when the ochre-brown, bell-shaped caps are dusted with similar-coloured, glistening, mica-like grains. The older caps lose these and the grooved margin often splits and turns up. The crowded pale gills age brown then black before dissolving into a black fluid. The white stem browns at its base.

Size	Cap 2-4 cm, stem 5-8 cm x 2-4 mm.
Habitat	In dense clusters on broad-leaved stumps and logs. Also from dead roots.
Season	Throughout the year.
Edible	Hardly worthwhile; poor flavour and texture.
Similar species	Frequently confused with Rusty Carpet Ink Cap (p.140) which has white grains and grows from a rust-coloured mat.

FAIRIES' BONNETS *Coprinus disseminatus*

This tiny fungus would probably pass unnoticed but for the fact that it grows in very large groups; often several hundred together. The young, oval-shaped, pale beige caps mature bell-shaped, markedly grooved and greyer, though the apex remains brown. The pale grey gills darken with age but show little of the autodigesting (dissolving to an inky fluid) of other Ink Caps. The spindly, fragile grey-white stem has a downy base.

Size	Cap 0.5-1.5 cm, stem 2-4 cm x 1-2 mm.
Habitat	Large clusters on and near rotting wood.
Season	Spring to early winter.
Edible	Too insubstantial to be worthwhile.
Similar species	The habit of growing in such large groups distinguishes it from other related species.

FAIRY PARASOL *Coprinus plicatilis*

A very delicate fungus common in short grass and unusual for an Ink Cap in having a cap which finally flattens and shrivels rather than dissolving to a black ink. Initially pale tan, the paper-thin, ribbed, translucent cap turns grey apart from a brown central disc. The thin, spaced, grey-black gills radiate from a collar round the easily broken, tall slender stem.

Size	Cap 1-2 cm, stem 4-6 cm x 2-3 mm.
Habitat	In short grass and among woodland herbs.
Season	Spring to early winter.
Edible	Far too insubstantial to be worth collecting.
Similar species	A number of related species, e.g. *C. leiocephalus*, have browner caps and are found beneath trees or in hedgerows.

COMMON CRUMBLE CAP *Psathyrella candolleana*

Only old caps show the dark gill and spore colour, so they are frequently confused with white and pink-spored species. This one has a thin-fleshed, ochre-yellow cap which soon flattens and dries pale cream, especially near the margin which frequently splits and bears dark veil remnants. The gills are crowded, adnexed and initially white then lilac-grey before turning dark brown. The cap does not dissolve. The stem is thin, white and brittle.

Size	Cap 3-6 cm, stem 5-8 cm x 3-5 mm.
Habitat	In tufts near broad-leaved tree stumps.
Season	Early summer to autumn.
Edible	Said to be edible if cooked but not worthwhile.
Similar species	There are many Crumble Caps; most grow in small groups on soil or among grass.

Two-Toned Crumble Cap *Psathyrella hydrophila*

A densely tufted species, common on stumps. The neatly convex young caps are a beautiful, shiny date-brown with small white veil fragments at the margins. As the cap ages it flattens and dries pale tan from the centre, giving a two-toned appearance. The young, pale brown, crowded gills blacken as the spores mature. The fragile, smooth white stem darkens near its base.

Size	Cap 2-5 cm, stem 4-8 cm x 5-8 mm.
Habitat	In dense clusters on broad-leaved tree stumps, dead roots and other debris.
Season	Early summer to late autumn.
Edible	Not recommended due to bitter taste.
Similar species	Brown Stew Fungus (p.115) is also tufted on stumps but has a ring and scaly brown stem base.

145

HAY CAP *Panaeolus foenisecii*

Like the previous species, this has a two-toned, brown, convex cap. As the picture shows some may be all date-brown and others much paler. The ascending pale brown gills later become mottled with black patches from the ripe spores. The stem is slender, smooth and brown. Also called *Panaeolina foenisecii*.

Size	Cap 1-2 cm, stem 4-6 cm x 2-3 mm.
Habitat	Among short and mown grass.
Season	Midsummer to autumn.
Poisonous	May produce hallucinations .
Similar species	*P. rickenii* has a bell-shaped, red-brown cap and a white bloom on its dark brown stem. Brown Bell Cap (p.111) has rusty-brown gills. Magic Mushroom (p.120) has a pointed cap and unmottled dark brown gills.

PETTICOAT FUNGUS *Panaeolus sphinctrinus*

A common small grassland species usually growing on dung, it gets its name from the cap margin which is fringed with triangular, white veil fragments. The deeply bell-shaped cap varies from grey to almost black when moist but dries grey-brown. The adnate brown gills are mottled with black patches (its alternative name is Grey Mottle Gill). The grey-brown, stem is long, slender and covered with a white bloom in the upper region.

Size	Cap 2-4 cm, stem 6-12 cm x 2-3 mm.
Habitat	In grazed grassland; on or near dung.
Season	Early summer to autumn.
Poisonous	May produce hallucinations.
Similar species	Some authors consider browner-capped specimens with fewer veil remains to be *P. campanulatus*.

EGG-SHELL TOADSTOOL *Panaeolus semiovatus*

Found on horse or cow dung, this is much larger than the two previous species in the same genus. The cap remains bell-shaped with an uneven surface. It is creamy-ochre; sticky when moist and shiny when dry – like an egg-shell. The ascending brown and black, mottled gills have a paler edge. The creamy-white stem bears a ring, later blackened by the spores.

Size	Cap 2-6 cm, stem 5-15 cm x 4-8 mm.
Habitat	On horse and cow dung or in gardens on manure.
Season	Summer to early winter.
Inedible	Its dung habitat makes it unsuitable for eating.
Similar species	Other common Panaeolus species are smaller, darker and lack a ring.

WEEPING WIDOW *Lacrymaria velutina*

The broadly convex yellow-brown cap maintains a central umbo. When young it is covered with darker fibres and has a shaggy margin due to veil fragments which blacken as the spores develop. The crowded adnate gills are mottled brown and black with a white edge. In moist weather watery droplets are exuded near the junction of gill and stem. The stem has brown fibres and a ring zone blackened by the spores. Listed in some books as *Psathyrella lacrymabunder*.

Size	Cap 5-10 cm, stem 6-10 cm x 6-10 mm.
Habitat	In lawns, grassy woods and bare soil in fields.
Season	Early summer to late autumn.
Poisonous	Firm-fleshed if a little bitter.
Similar species	Common Crumble Cap (p.144) is much paler.

CEP *Boletus edulis*

Cep or Penny Bun has densely-packed tubes in place of gills. The young, deeply convex caps are often wrinkled and narrower than the broad stem but expand to a large, fleshy, shallow dome-shape. The cap is mid-brown with paler patches and sticky when moist. The pores (tube ends) are small and white, ageing straw to olive-yellow. The very swollen pale brown stem is overlain by a raised, white honeycomb network most obvious at the apex.

Size	Cap 8-30 cm, stem 8-25 cm x 4-10 cm.
Habitat	Woodlands; with oak, beech, birch and pine.
Season	Early summer to autumn.
Edible	Young ones can be pickled. Old ones dry well.
Similar species	See Bay Bolete (p.151) and Bitter Bolete (p.157).

150

BAY BOLETE *Boletus badius*

Also known as *Xerocomus badius*. The cap is shiny, chestnut or bay-horse coloured; it is sticky and darker when wet. Cylindrical stem, streaked with cap colour. The pores are large, angular and pale yellow, rapidly turning blue-green on bruising. The pale yellow flesh blues faintly when cut.

Size	Cap 7-15 cm, stem 5-12 cm x 20-25 mm.
Habitat	Broad-leaved or coniferous (especially Scots pine) wood on acid soil.
Season	July to November.
Edible	Excellent and firm-fleshed when young. Pleasant mushroomy taste. Rarely maggot-infested. Dries well.
Similar species	Red-cracked Bolete and Yellow-cracked Bolete (pp.152 &153). The paler Cep (p.150) has a raised network on its broader stem.

RED-CRACKED BOLETE *Boletus chrysenteron*

A very common Bolete, also known as *Xerocomus chrysenteron* with a shallowly convex yellow-brown, dry cap which later cracks to reveal a pink-red layer just below the surface. The large, angular yellow pores age olive and bruise blue-green. The cylindrical stem is pale yellow at its apex but flushed red towards the base.

Size	Cap 5-10 cm, stem 4-8 cm x 10-15 mm.
Habitat	Under broad-leaved trees in woods and gardens.
Season	Midsummer to late autumn.
Edible	Not recommended due to its soggy texture.
Similar species	Yellow-cracked Bolete (p.153) has no red on the stem or beneath the cracks on the cap. *Boletus pruinatus* has a red-brown cap with smaller, pale yellow pores which bruise blue.

YELLOW-CRACKED BOLETE *Boletus subtomentosus*

This species, often placed in the genus *Xerocomus* has a pale olive-yellow to light brown, dry cap with a velvety feel. At maturity the surface cracks to reveal the pale yellow flesh. The golden-yellow, angular pores are larger close to the stem and age olive-yellow. It blues faintly when bruised. The creamy-yellow stem often bends and narrows near its base.

Size	Cap 3-10 cm, stem 4-10 cm x 10-20 mm.
Habitat	Under broad-leaved and coniferous trees.
Season	Summer to late autumn.
Edible	Not recommended due to its poor flavour and a soggy texture.
Similar species	A very variable species and darker forms look like Bay Bolete (p.151) while some forms look like Red-cracked Bolete (p.152).

DOTTED-STEMMED BOLETE *Boletus erythropus*

A large, solid Bolete with yellow flesh in the cap
and stem which rapidly turns dark blue on cutting.
The fleshy, broadly convex cap is usually dark olive-
brown with a velvet surface when young; later
smooth and glossy. The small, round yellow pores
mature deep orange-red and bruise dark blue. The
yellow, club-shaped stem bruises blue and is covered
with tiny red-brown dots in the lower region.

Size	Cap 8-20 cm, stem 6-12 cm x 20-40 mm.
Habitat	Under broad-leaved or coniferous trees, commonly on neutral or acidic soils.
Season	Early summer to autumn.
Poisonous	Causes stomach upset especially when raw.
Similar species	Lurid and Devil's Bolete (see p.155).

LURID BOLETE *Boletus luridus*

The yellow-brown fleshy cap bears tubes with orange-red pores which, like the cap, stem and cut flesh, bruise blue-green. The broad stem is yellowish at the top but most of the rest is covered by a purple-red, longitudinally elongated net.

Size	Cap 8-14 cm, stem 5-12 cm x 15-40 mm.
Habitat	Under beech, oak or lime on chalky soils.
Season	Midsummer to autumn.
Poisonous	Causes digestive upset and produces unpleasant symptoms with alcohol.
Similar species	Devil's Bolete (*Boletus satanus*) has a large creamy-brown, wavy-margined cap. Small yellow-red pores bruise blue-green, cut flesh smells unpleasant and slowly blues, stem has a very swollen base and a red net. Causes severe sickness but is not fatal.

PARASITIC BOLETE *Boletus parasiticus*

This small, infrequent Bolete is instantly recognisable as it is always found attached to Common Earth Ball (see p.219) which it parasitises. The pale, olive-brown dry cap is initially velvety but cracks on maturity. The margin remains inrolled until old. The large, angular, golden-yellow pores age red-brown. The yellow-brown stem often narrows at its base and curves from the underside of its earthball host. Also known as *Xerocomus parasiticus*.

Size	Cap 2-5 cm, stem 3-6 cm x 8-12 mm.
Habitat	Singly or in small tufts on Common Earthball.
Season	Autumn.
Edible	Not recommended as it is quite rare.
Similar species	None; the only parasitic Bolete.

BITTER BOLETE *Tylopilus felleus*

A frequent species which when young can be mistaken for Cep (p.150). The domed mid-brown cap has a wavy edge which often overlaps the marginal tubes. The tiny white pores turn flesh-pink as the spores mature. The club-shaped, pale ochre stem is covered with a brown raised honeycomb network. The white cap flesh is odourless but tastes very bitter.

Size	Cap 5-14 cm, stem 6-14 cm x 20-40 mm.
Habitat	Under both conifers and broad-leaved species (especially beech and oak), often on acid soils.
Season	Summer to autumn.
Inedible	Extremely bitter taste.
Similar species	Cep (p.150) is a similar colour but the pores age olive-yellow and the stem bears a white network.

157

PEPPERY BOLETE *Chalciporus piperatus*

Previously known as *Boletus piperatus*, it is smaller than most common Boletes. The orange-brown, smooth cap is slightly sticky when moist but frequently cracks when dry and has a wavy margin. The cap flesh is yellow. The small rusty-brown pores are larger and more angular close to the stem which is often off-centre to the cap. The stem is red-brown, narrowing markedly to a bright yellow base.

Size	Cap 3-6 cm, stem 3-8 cm x 8-15 mm.
Habitat	Common under birch or pine on sandy soil. Also with beech and oak.
Season	Late summer to late autumn.
Edible	Used to add flavour but is very peppery.
Similar species	None with such a hot taste.

ORANGE BIRCH BOLETE *Leccinum versipelle*

Species of *Leccinum* differ from *Boletus* in having tiny scales on a longer stem. When young, *versipelle* has a rounded, firm, brick-red cap; this matures to a large, convex, orange-brown, dry cap, often with a shaggy edge. The pores are small, round and dirty white; they age pale brown. The long stem tapers from a swollen base; white, covered by small brown or black scales. The firm, pale pink flesh turns blue-grey when cut and black on cooking.

Size Cap 12-25 cm, stem 12-20 cm x 30-40 mm.

Habitat Under birch in open woods and scrub.

Season Early summer to autumn, often after rain.

Edible Caps make good eating; discard the stems.

Similar Less common species with red-brown stem scales

species grow with oak, aspen and poplar.

BROWN BIRCH BOLETE *Leccinum scabrum*

Commoner than the preceding species with a dull, grey-brown smaller, spongy-textured cap and no overhanging margin. The tubes round the stem are much shorter than elsewhere. The tiny grey pores bruise pale brown. The cylindrical white stem is peppered with tiny brown-black scales. The white, soft flesh does not change colour on cutting or cooking.

Size	Cap 5-10 cm, stem 8-15 cm x 20-30 mm.
Habitat	Under birch; locally abundant.
Season	Early summer to autumn.
Edible	Soggy. Only young caps are worth eating.
Similar species	Easily confused with Orange Birch Bolete (p.159); this is larger, firmer and has flesh that blues on cutting. *L. roseofractum* has a dark brown cap and flesh that turns dark pink on cutting.

160

LARCH BOLETE *Suillus grevillei*

Species of *Suillus* are distinguished from those of *Boletus* or *Leccinum* by their slimy caps and larger pore size. Larch Bolete (was *Boletus elegans*) has a slimy, golden-yellow cap which dries glossy. The pores are large, angular and initially covered by a pale yellow veil which forms a ring on the stem. This drops off, leaving a paler area above which the yellow stem is scurfy.

Size	Cap 4-12 cm, stem 5-10 cm x 12-18 mm.
Habitat	Under or close to larch, often in rings.
Season	Summer to late autumn.
Edible	Remove slimy cap skin. Best in soups.
Similar species	*S. aeruginascens* has a wrinkled, grey-yellow cap; *S. tridentinus* has compound orange pores. Slippery Jack (p.162) is brown and grows under pine.

SLIPPERY JACK *Suillus luteus*

The only common slimy-capped Bolete with a persistent ring. The chestnut-brown cap finally dries smooth and shiny. The yellow pores are initially covered with a white veil; they brown with age and on bruising. The stem is pale yellow and scurfy above the floppy ring; creamy-brown below. The flesh is pale yellow and soft.

Size	Cap 6-12 cm, stem 5-10 cm x 15-20 mm.
Habitat	Under pine trees on well-drained soil.
Season	Late summer to autumn.
Edible	Remove slimy skin. Lacks flavour.
Similar species	Related species growing under pine include Shallow-pored Bolete (p.163) and *S. granulatus*: both lack a ring and the latter exudes milky droplets from its pores and granular stem.

Shallow-pored Bolete *Suillus bovinus*

As the common name suggests, this has a thin cap; the Latin name refers to the oxen or Jersey cow-like colour of the slimy cap which dries shiny with a paler margin. The large, angular, olive-yellow pores are frequently subdivided and are elongated near the stem where the tubes are slightly decurrent. The smooth cap-coloured, cylindrical stem lacks a ring and often bends at the base.

Size	Cap 4-12 cm, stem 4-10 cm x 10-15 mm.
Habitat	In grass, moss and heather under Scots pine.
Season	Late summer to autumn.
Edible	Poor flavour and rubbery texture.
Similar species	The larger, yellower Larch Bolete (p.161) grows with larch. Peppery Bolete (p.158) grows with pine but has a dry, matt cap and a peppery taste.

BROWN ROLL-RIM *Paxillus involutus*

The very common Brown Roll-rim has a convex young cap which finally becomes flat and even funnel-shaped but retains a shaggy inrolled margin. The soft gills are easily removed from the cap, which is olive to rust-brown and slimy at the centre when moist. It bruises darker as do the very crowded, decurrent, forking brown gills and the pale brown stem which narrows from the apex.

Size	Cap 7-15 cm, stem 4-8 cm x 10-20 mm.
Habitat	Under broad-leaved trees in woods and heaths; often with birch. Locally abundant.
Season	Midsummer to late autumn.
Poisonous	Causes sickness and more serious illness.
Similar species	See Velvet Roll-rim (p.165).

Velvet Roll-Rim *Paxillus atromentosus*

In contrast to Brown Roll-rim this is a wood rotter and grows on old conifer stumps. The large, chunky, irregular cap has a semicircular or shell-like outline. It is flat or centrally depressed, with an inrolled, smooth margin. The dingy brown surface is dry and velvety when young, smoother with age. The decurrent crowded, creamy-yellow gills fork near the short broad, velvety, brown-black stem which is often laterally attached.

Size	Cap 8-25 cm, stem 4-8 cm x 20-50 mm.
Habitat	Clustered on or near conifer stumps, mostly on pine.
Season	Midsummer to autumn.
Poisonous	Bitter and similar to Brown Roll-rim.
Similar species	Brown Roll-rim (see p.164).

165

FALSE CHANTERELLE *Hygrophoropsis aurantiaca*

Frequently mistaken for Chanterelle (p.167) despite growing in different habitats. The dry, rather downy, funnel-shaped cap has an inrolled margin and depressed centre. Thin-fleshed, the whole fruitbody is orange-yellow but dries darker. It also occurs as a paler variety. The decurrent gills are thin, crowded and frequently forked. The slender stem is often off-centre, narrowing to the base which often curves.

Size	Cap 3-8 cm, stem 2-5 cm x 5-8 mm.
Habitat	Mostly under conifers or on acid heaths.
Season	Late summer to late autumn.
Poisonous	A minority suffer from sickness and hallucinations.
Similar species	Chanterelle (p.167) has a paler, chunkier cap and stem with shallow wrinkles instead of gills.

CHANTERELLE *Cantharellus cibarius*

Chanterelle is collected for its culinary value. The convex cap, thick-fleshed and egg-yolk yellow, expands flat and finally funnel-shaped with an inrolled, wavy margin. It has coloured, blunt-edged deep wrinkles, with cross veins, which divide and reunite. These replace the normal gills and run down on to a solid stem. It has a fruity smell.

Size	Cap 2-10 cm, stem 2-8 cm x 8-20 mm.
Habitat	Under broad-leaved trees (e.g beech, oak, or birch), also under pine; often among moss on slopes.
Season	Summer to autumn.
Edible	Mildly peppery taste goes well with egg dishes. Can be eaten raw. Small ones pickle well.
Similar species	See False Chanterelle (p.166).

TUBED CHANTERELLE *Cantharellus tubaeformis*

This occasional species grows in troops, mostly under conifers. Previously called *C.infundibuliformis* it has a depressed, navel-like cap which, unlike Chanterelle, is thin-fleshed, lacks an inrolled margin and is usually yellow-brown. The decurrent, forked wrinkles (in place of gills) start yellow but mature orange-grey and run on to the tall, slender, hollow, flattened, orange-yellow stem. There is little or no smell.

Size	Cap 2-5 cm, stem 5-8 cm x 5-10 mm.
Habitat	In troops, mostly under conifers.
Season	Autumn.
Edible	A poorer version of Chanterelle.
Similar species	Yellow forms look like Chanterelle (p.167) but this has a solid stem and fleshier cap.

HORN OF PLENTY *Craterellus cornucopoides*

The cap of this strange fungus is shaped like a trumpet's horn with a split, wavy, rolled edge. The inside is dingy-brown while on the outer (under) surface there are no gills, the black leathery surface turning pale grey as the spores mature. The stem is merely a hollow extension of the tube-like cap. Also called Trumpet of Death.

Size	Cap and stem 2-8 cm wide, 4-10 cm tall.
Habitat	In troops among leaf litter of beech or oak.
Season	Summer to early winter.
Edible	A favourite in restaurants where it is served stuffed, but it is leathery and best used dried to add a rich flavour to soups and stews.
Similar species	The much rarer *C. cinereus* differs in producing spores from black, Chanterelle-like wrinkles.

OYSTER MUSHROOM *Pleurotus ostreatus*

Increasingly cultivated, its flat, moist, slate-blue or oyster-coloured caps are fan-shaped with an inrolled margin. They dry grey-buff or cream. Decurrent crowded, white to pale straw gills radiate from the point of attachment where they may fork. Small lateral stem, downy when young.

Size	Cap 5-18 cm, stem 2-3 cm x 10-20 mm.
Habitat	In overlapping clusters on living trunks, dead stumps and logs of broad-leaved trees; rare on conifers.
Season	Late autumn and through the winter.
Edible	Good flavour and firm-fleshed. Cut out stem area.
Similar species	*P. pulmonarius* is less substantial. See next two pages for species which can be confused with Oyster Mushroom.

Branched Oyster Mushroom *Pleurotus cornucopiae*

The round or oval caps are creamy-brown and darker at the depressed centre. The significant stem is attached nearer to one side of the cap and is almost covered by a continuation of the off-white gills. These regularly fork and reunite over the stem which fuses with many others at its base.

Size	Cap 5-12 cm, stem 2-7 cm x 15-30 mm.
Habitat	Clustered on dead elm; also on beech.
Season	Summer to early autumn.
Edible	Tougher and less tasty than Oyster Mushroom.
Similar species	*P. dryinus* mostly on oak with a scaly cap and marginal veil fragments. Oyster Mushroom (p.170) is greyer and lacks the significant branched stem and reuniting gills. It fruits later in the year.

OLIVE-BROWN PANELLUS *Panellus serotinus*

The fan- or kidney-shaped, fleshy cap has an inrolled margin when young. The colour varies; it is initially yellow-orange then olive-green and finally (especially after frost) bronze-brown. It is slimy when moist but dries velvety. The crowded orange-yellow gills are darker near the short, broad, yellow-brown, felty, lateral stem.

Size	Cap 3-12 cm, stem 1-2 cm x 10-20 mm.
Habitat	Overlapping tufts on stumps and dead wood of both broad-leaved (e.g.beech) and coniferous trees.
Season	From late autumn through the winter.
Inedible	Slimy cap may cause digestive upset.
Similar species	*P. stipticus* has small, dry, brown caps. See also Oyster Mushroom (p,170).

SOFT SLIPPER TOADSTOOL *Crepidotus mollis*

The common name refers to its soft texture; the Latin name reminds us of the pancake-like shape of this bracket-like fungus. The pale brown, kidney-shaped cap, with a slimy covering and grooved margin, dries smooth and cream-coloured. The crowded white gills fan out and turn brown as the spores mature. The stem is lateral or absent.

Size	Cap 2-7 cm across, (no stem).
Habitat	Overlapping tiers on dead trunks and stumps of broad-leaved trees.
Season	Early summer to late autumn.
Inedible	Insubstantial and slimy textured.
Similar species	Can be confused with Oyster Mushroom (p.170) but this is much larger and has white gills. Olive-brown Panellus (p.172) has yellow gills.

ORANGE CLUBS *Clavulinopsis helvola*

This is one of the commonest of a group of grassland fungi with club-shaped fruitbodies the size of a matchstick. The unbranched, orange-yellow club is flattened near the rounded apex and narrows to the base. The spores are borne on the smooth surface.

Size	2-6 cm tall, 2-4 mm wide.
Habitat	In short grass, often among moss. Also among herbs in broad-leaved woods. In small groups.
Season	Midsummer to autumn.
Inedible	Insubstantial with a bitter taste.
Similar species	Golden Spindles (*Clavulinopsis fusiformis*), taller and bright yellow, has pointed tips. *Clavulinopsis corniculata* has branched yellow clubs. White Spindles (*Clavaria vermicularis*) is tufted and unbranched.

CRESTED CORAL FUNGUS *Clavulina cristata*

Clavulina and *Ramaria* species have branched, coral-like fruitbodies. This, the commonest species is usually white, densely branched and with flattened branches ending in pointed, crest-like tips. It is soft and easily broken. Darker forms with greyer tips are confusable with Grey Coral Fungus (p.176).

Size	2-8 cm tall, 2-6 cm wide.
Habitat	Solitary or gregarious on soil. Often among leaf litter under broad-leaved or coniferous trees.
Season	Midsummer to autumn.
Edible	Not recommended as often infected with mould.
Similar species	Grey Coral Fungus (p.176). The larger, rarer, pale pink *Ramaria botrytis* is more finely branched and has deep red, bitter-tasting tips.

GREY CORAL FUNGUS *Clavulina cinerea*

This is very similar to the previous species but slightly larger and the much branched, coral-like fruitbody is grey-brown. The branches are often flattened and the ends are blunt or rounded but not pointed.

Size	3-10 cm tall, 2-8 cm wide.
Habitat	In broad-leaved or coniferous woods, usually among leaf litter. Solitary or in small groups.
Season	Midsummer to late autumn.
Edible	Insubstantial and not recommended.
Similar species	Often difficult to separate from Crested Coral Fungus (p.175) which usually has pointed branch ends. The rare *Thelephora palmata* has more purple-brown branches and a strong smell of onion.

CAULIFLOWER FUNGUS *Sparassis crispa*

Similar in size and appearance to a human brain or cauliflower, the fruitbody is composed of many vertical, flattened, leaf-like lobes. When young and brittle these are cream-coloured with pale yellow tips but they age brown and tougher. The fleshy basal stem is often partly buried and root-like. It has a slightly sweet smell and tastes of hazelnuts.

Size	10-20 cm tall, 15-40 cms wide.
Habitat	On the ground close to living trunks or dead stumps of conifers; mostly with Scots pine.
Season	Late summer to autumn.
Edible	Young, well-washed specimens have a marvellous taste and texture. Must not be eaten when old.
Similar species	Hen of the Woods (p.200) has horizontal lobes with pores on the underside and grows on or near oak.

177

HEDGEHOG FUNGUS *Hydnum repandum*

This species has spines (stalagtite-like projections) from the cap in place of gills. It has a medium-sized, fleshy, creamy-buff cap with an inrolled, often wavy or irregular margin. Neighbouring caps may coalesce. The spines are paler than the cap, crowded, brittle and continuing on to the top of the short stocky stem which is often not centrally attached.

Size	Cap 6-14 cm, stem 4-6 cm x 15-25 mm.
Habitat	Under both broad-leaved (especially beech) and coniferous trees; often in troops.
Season	Autumn.
Edible	Slightly bitter when raw but excellent after cooking, with a firm texture.
Similar species	*H. rufescens* is smaller and more orange-red.

EAR-PICK FUNGUS *Auriscalpium vulgare*

A curious little fungus growing on old pine cones. The thin dark brown cap is shaped like an ear and the convex surface is coarsely velvety and often channelled to the laterally attached stem. In place of gills there are tiny (2-3 mm), grey-brown spines which hang down like stalagtites. The slender, cap-coloured stem has a bristly surface.

Size	Cap 1-2 cm, stem 2-6 cm x 1-2 mm.
Habitat	Singly or in small groups on decaying (often buried) cones of pine and occasionally spruce.
Season	Mostly autumn but appearing all year.
Inedible	Insubstantial and tough.
Similar species	Two other common fungi fruit on cones - *Strobilurus esculentus* (spring) and *Baeospora myosura* (autumn) but these have gills, not spines.

EARTH FAN *Thelephora terrestris*

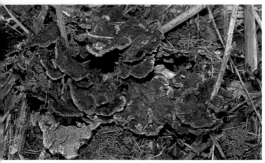

With no cap, stem or gills, its fruitbody consists of flattened, soft, grey-brown, fan-shaped lobes which frequently fuse to give a rosette appearance. The lobes are either semi-erect in a shallow bowl-shape or flat and encrusting twigs and plant stems. The upper surface is radially zoned and felty with a paler, irregularly fringed margin. The smooth, lower spore-bearing surface is cinnamon-brown and wrinkled.

Size	In patches, 3-20 cm across.
Habitat	On soil or needle litter under conifers; also under broad-leaved trees and on heaths.
Season	Summer to late autumn.
Inedible	Insubstantial
Similar species	Hairy Stereum (p.181) grows on wood.

Hairy Stereum *Stereum hirsutum*

This forms encrustations and rows of small, thin, tough semicircular bracket-like caps which frequently fuse with their neighbours. The zoned upper-side is roughly hairy and ranges from yellow-orange to grey-brown (frequently green with algae when old). The paler, broader, undulating margin is hairless. The lower, spore-bearing surface is smooth and initially bright yellow-orange but fades grey-brown.

Size	Individual caps are 2-6 cm across, 2-3 mm thick.
Habitat	Tiered on stumps, dead standing and fallen wood of broad-leaved trees; also on posts and other timbers.
Season	Throughout the year.
Inedible	Tough and leathery
Similar species	Bleeding Stereum (p.182). Many-zoned Polypore (p.185) has tiny pores on its creamy underside.

181

BLEEDING STEREUM *Stereum rugosum*

Bleeding Stereum is usually found as a hard flat crust which forms large patches on dead wood. The margins occasionally turn up to form tiny brackets. The pale ochre surface is initially smooth and flat but becomes uneven and may crack when dry. Fresh specimens bruise red and bleed a red juice when scratched; hence the common name.

Size	Patches 2-20 cm across, only 1-2 mm thick.
Habitat	Crusts on dead wood of broad-leaved trees especially hazel, birch, beech and oak.
Season	Throughout the year.
Inedible	Hard and tough.
Similar species	Other bleeders include the red-brown *S. gausapatum* on oak; it regularly forms small brackets and *S.sanguinolentum* which grows on coniferous wood.

SILVER LEAF FUNGUS *Chondrostereum purpureum*

This species occurs as a flat crust which turns up to produce small, leathery bracket-like caps. These have faintly zoned, hairy, pale grey upper surfaces with pale undulating margins. When young the underside, like the crust region, is smooth or finely wrinkled and a striking pink-violet colour, fading to dark brown. Previously called *Stereum purpureum*.

Size	Patches to 15 cm across, brackets 2-4 cm across.
Habitat	Tiered on dead wood of broad-leaved trees. On living wood of rowan and fruit trees where it causes 'silver leaf'.
Season	Throughout the year.
Inedible	Very tough.
Similar species	Violet Fir Bracket (see p.184) has pores and grows on conifers.

VIOLET FIR BRACKET *Trichaptum abietinum*

Previously known as *Hirschioporus abietinus*, its small thin brackets grow in many-layered tiers on dead conifer wood. The upper surface is hairy, grey-brown, undulating, concentrically zoned and grooved. It may turn green from entrapped algae. The margin and pored underside is bright violet when young but fades to chocolate-brown. The pores become more elongated with age.

Size	Patches to 30 cm x 30 cm. Brackets 2-4 cm aross.
Habitat	Overlapping tiers on dead conifer wood including sawn logs. Mostly on larch, pine, spruce and fir.
Season	Throughout the year.
Inedible	Insubstantial and tough.
Similar species	The purple-tinged Silver Leaf Fungus (p.183) is smooth below and grows on broad-leaved trees.

Many-zoned Polypore *Coriolus versicolor*

Very common, with semicircular or kidney-shaped thin, leathery brackets. The upper wrinkled surface is slightly hairy and shows contrasting concentric zones of black, grey and brown with a paler, undulating margin. The pored underside is creamy-white to pale ochre. Also called *Trametes versicolor*.

Size	2-7 cm across, 2-5 cm broad x 1-5 mm thick.
Habitat	On stumps, logs and standing dead wood. Also on living wood; mostly on broad-leaved trees. Usually in large overlapping groups.
Season	Throughout the year.
Inedible	Like dried leather.
Similar species	The pale tan *C. hirsuta* is less clearly zoned and more hairy. See also Hairy Stereum (p.181).

GREY POLYPORE *Bjerkandera adusta*

This forms crust-like patches on the underside of branches but many overlapping, thin, pliable brackets on upper or vertical surfaces. The grey-brown bracket is faintly zoned with a whitish margin which ages black. The pored underside is pale grey, with a white margin but blackens on bruising and with age.

Size	Brackets 2-6 cm across, 4-7 mm thick.
Habitat	Tiered on dead wood and damaged areas of broad-leaved trees, especially on beech.
Season	Throughout the year.
Inedible	With a leathery texture.
Similar species	The dark grey pores help distinguish this species from other small brackets including *B. fumosa* which has cream-coloured pores.

JELLY ROT *Merulius tremellosus*

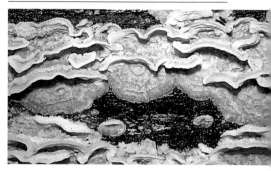

This strange, soft bracket has a moist gelatinous texture. It can be pancake-like but usually forms small brackets at its margins. The thick felty upperside is creamy-white with a pink tinge and has a thinner, almost tranlucent margin. The underside appears to be pored but is in fact a mix of folds and deep wrinkles. It is a striking orange-pink when fresh.

Size	Individual brackets 2-4 cm across but frequently coalescing.
Habitat	Rotten wood on stumps and fallen trunks. Mostly on broad-leaved trees.
Season	Commonest in summer and autumn.
Inedible	Soft but insubstantial.
Similar species	*Phlebia radiata* forms soft, grey, wrinkled crusts with bright orange edges.

ROOT FOMES *Heterobasidion annosum*

A serious parasite of conifers, especially spruce, the fruitbodies are formed from the lower trunk/upper root zone where the brackets are often partly hidden by moss and grass. It is crust-like but also produces small, irregular, elongated lobes. These are dark brown to black, with a hard lumpy surface and a wavy margin showing the white of the underside which is covered with small angular pores. If cut open older fruitbodies show annual layers of tubes.

Size	Up to 15 cm across, 8 cm broad and 4 cm thick.
Habitat	With conifers; mostly at the base of spruce trees.
Season	Throughout the year as it is perennial.
Inedible	Very hard.
Similar species	None in the same habitat.

HUMP-BACKED POLYPORE *Pseudotrametes gibbosa*

This medium-sized fungus forms semicircular brackets which are much thicker and humped at their point of attachment. The white upper side has a slightly velvety lumpy surface. Old specimens become browner and are frequently green in the middle from encrusting algae. The creamy-white pores on the underside are unusual in being elongated into thick-walled slots. Also called *Trametes gibbosa*.

Size	10-20 cm across, 6-15 cm broad, 1-5 cm thick.
Habitat	On dead broad-leaved trees.
Season	Throughout the year.
Inedible	Tough even when young.
Similar species	Blushing Bracket (p.190) has a thinner, brown bracket with pores that bruise pink on handling.

BLUSHING BRACKET *Daedaleopsis confragosa*

A medium-sized fungus with a semicircular-shaped, tough fruitbody with an uneven, concentrically zoned, radially streaked, ochre-brown upper side; paler at the margin. The white underside ages grey-brown but bruises dark pink-red. The large pores are round and angular, some slit-like others maze-like.

Size	4-14 cm across, 4-8 cm broad, 1-3 cm thick.
Habitat	On living or dead broad-leaved trunks and branches. Mostly on willow and alder.
Season	Throughout the year.
Inedible	Tough, becoming woody.
Similar species	Hump-backed Polypore (p.189) also has elongated pores but a whiter, more uneven upperside and it does not flush red when bruised.

MAZE GILL *Daedalea quercina*

Commonest on oak stumps, this hard, corky bracket is unusually thick at its point of attachment. Above it is grey-brown and uneven. Below, the beige pores are greatly elongated (the walls appearing like thick gills) and form a labyrinth or maze-like pattern. (In Greek mythology Daedalus had to find his way through a labyrinth.)

Size	8-16 cm across, 4-8 cm broad, 2-5 cm thick.
Habitat	On dead wood of oak; rare on sweet chestnut.
Season	Throughout the year.
Inedible	Has a very hard texture.
Similar species	The smaller, thinner *Lenzites betulina* grows mostly on birch. The creamy-ochre underside has much thinner, more regular, gill-like plates.

BIRCH POLYPORE *Piptoporus betulinus*

A very common parasite on birch which continues
to grow on the dead wood. White, smooth and
rounded when young, it later develops a convex,
kidney or semicircular shape. It is thicker at the
lateral point of attachment, which is narrow and
stem-like. The white upper side ages brown or grey
and often cracks. The margin remains inrolled until
maturity. The white underside is punctuated with
tiny round pores. Also known as Razor Strop Fungus.

Size	8-30 cm across, 5-20 cm broad, 2-6 cm thick.
Habitat	On trunks and branches of living or dead birch.
Season	Throughout the year. Fruitbodies persist.
Inedible	The tough flesh has a bitter taste.
Similar species	See Hoof Fungus (p.193) - also on birch.

HOOF FUNGUS *Fomes fomentarius*

A very hard, broadly attached, perennial fruitbody; successive annual layers of tubes produce a hoof-like shape often as deep as it is wide. The upper side is smooth, pale grey with darker concentric bands and ridged with concentric furrows. It has a very broad, rounded margin. The underside has minute pores, initially pale grey-brown but later dark brown. The pale brown leathery flesh was used when lighting fires; hence its other name - Tinder Fungus.

Size	7-40 cm across, 5-20 cm broad, 7-20 cm deep.
Habitat	On dead or dying birch; also on beech.
Season	Any time - fruitbodies live for many years.
Inedible	As tough as the wood it grows on!
Similar species	*Phellinus igniarius* has a black, cracked 'hoof' and rusty-brown flesh. On willow; not common.

193

DRYAD'S SADDLE *Polyporus squamosus*

The large cap is semicircular or saddle-shaped (in Greek mythology dryads were wood nymphs), occasionally circular. It is flat-topped or depressed near the lateral or off-centred stem. The upper side is tan-yellow with concentric bands of dark brown, flat scales. The underside has large, angular creamy-yellow pores. The tubes run on to the thick stem which has a brown-black, velvety base.

Size	Cap to 50 cm x 5 cm thick, stem 3-10 cm x 1-6 cm.
Habitat	Overlapping clusters on broad-leaved trees including elm, beech and sycamore.
Season	Spring to summer. Not persisting.
Edible	Edges of young caps are the most tender.
Similar species	*P. tuberaster* is small and funnel-shaped.

SHAGGY POLYPORE *Inonotus hispidus*

The thick, broad-edged, semicircular brackets have a red-brown (later black), coarsely hairy upper side. The margin remains a brighter yellow-brown colour. The underside is pale yellow, maturing brown with small pores which often exude clear, dew-like drops. The cap is soft and moist when young; it dries tougher.

Size	10-25 cm across, 8-20 cm broad, 4-10 cm thick.
Habitat	Solitary or in small groups on trunks of broad-leaved trees; most frequently on ash.
Season	Summer but persisting through the year.
Inedible	Tough and often insect-ridden.
Similar species	*I. dryadeus* grows near the base of oak and the non-shaggy bracket exudes orange-red droplets.

COMMON GANODERMA *Ganoderma adspersum*

The very woody, perennial brackets consist of several layers of tubes; the lower layers are broader than the upper, above which is thick, dark brown flesh. The upper side is crust-like, with dark brown bumps and concentric ridges. The edge is rounded. The tiny creamy-grey pores on the underside bruise brown.

Size	10-30 cm across, 10-25 cm broad, 4-8 cm thick.
Habitat	Near the base of living trunks and dead stumps; mostly on broad-leaved trees, e.g. beech and lime.
Season	All year as the brackets are perennial.
Inedible	As hard as wood.
Similar species	Much confused with *G. applanatum* which is more sharp-edged and has thin, white-flecked, brown flesh.

BEEFSTEAK FUNGUS *Fistulina hepatica*

More like an ox tongue in shape, colour and texture, this strange fungus is soft and moist when young, with a rough pinky-red upper side and a broad margin. Older ones are firmer, smooth and liver-brown with a sharper edge. The straw-yellow pores bruise and age red-brown, often exuding a blood-red juice. The watery tubes are readily separated from the thick flesh which has the appearance of raw steak.

Size	8-20 cm across, 3-6 cm thick.
Habitat	Usually low on the trunk of old living oak and sweet chestnut trees; also on their stumps.
Season	Late summer to autumn; not persisting.
Edible	Best simmered; it can be bitter.
Similar species	None.

SULPHUR POLYPORE *Laetiporus sulphureus*

When young the fan-shaped brackets are soft and moist, with a broad margin. Old brackets become sharp-edged with a dry, chalky texture. Initially the upperside is bright orange or sulphur-yellow and has a suede-like feel but this fades to creamy-yellow with a smooth dry surface. The tiny round pores on the underside are pale yellow. It is thick-fleshed with a pleasant taste. Also known as Chicken of the Woods.

Size	Individual caps 5-20 cm across, 2-6 cm thick.
Habitat	Tiered on oak, sweet chestnut, yew and beech.
Season	Summer to early autumn. Occasionally persisting.
Edible	Texture of chicken but can cause nausea.
Similar species	Pale specimens of Giant Polypore (p.199) look similar but the pores bruise black.

GIANT POLYPORE *Meripilus giganteus*

Produces clusters of overlapping brackets up to a metre across. Each fan-shaped lobe arises from a common bulbous base. Tan-brown, radially wrinkled and faintly zoned with fine, darker brown fibres. The undulating thin margin often divides into smaller sub-brackets. The small-pored cream underside blackens on handling as does the flesh.

Size	Lobes 10-35 cm across, 1-3 cm thick.
Habitat	On stumps, roots or near the base of living broad-leaved trees; mostly on beech.
Season	Summer to early autumn. Soon rotting.
Edible	Slow-cooked young brackets are edible but can cause gastric upset in some people.
Similar species	Can be confused with Sulphur Polypore (p.198), Dryad's Saddle (p.194) and Hen of the Woods (p.200).

HEN OF THE WOODS *Grifola frondosa*

Typically found at the base of oak, it forms a cauliflower-like rosette of small, soft, horizontal, grey-brown, leafy brackets which branch from a central white stem. Each thin, undulating, fan-shaped segment is radially furrowed. The small round pores on the underside continue to the top of the stem. The sweet smell becomes less pleasant as it ages.

Size	Whole fruitbody up to 40 cm in diameter.
Habitat	On stumps, roots and at the base of living broad-leaved trees; mostly with oak.
Season	Autumn. Not persisting.
Edible	Slow cooking softens the tough texture.
Similar species	Has been confused with Giant Polypore (p.199) and Cauliflower Fungus (p.177) - the latter grows at the base of conifers.

FUZZY POLYPORE *Phaeolus schweinitzii*

The mature fruitbody is shaped like a broad inverted cone. The flat top is initially rusty-orange, convex and concentrically grooved. It is soft and spongy when young, with a fuzzy, mat-like surface. It ages dry, dark red-brown to black with a paler edge. The olive-yellow pores become maze-like and turn brown with age and handling. The tubes run onto the stocky brown stem.

Size	Cap 8-30 cm diameter, stem 3-8 cm x 2-6 cm.
Habitat	On stumps or from the roots of conifers, including pine, spruce and larch. Solitary.
Season	Autumn. Dried specimens persist into winter.
Inedible	Often encrusts old pine needles.
Similar species	None.

BROWN GOBLET *Coltricia perennis*

Growing on the ground, this species is easy to mistake for a toadstool but it has a thin, tough, corky cap with tubes on its underside. The circular cap is flat or funnel-shaped and velvety, with concentric yellow-brown, rust and grey-brown bands which give it the appearance of tree rings. The pale thin undulating edge often splits. The pores are rusty-brown, angular and decurrent on to the narrow, frequently flattened, velvety brown stem.

Size	Cap 3-7 cm, stem 2-5 cm x 3-8 mm.
Habitat	On well-drained or burnt ground; often under pine.
Season	Late summer but old fruitbodies persist.
Inedible	However, it is used in floral decorations.
Similar species	Winter Polypore (*Polyporus brumalis*) lacks the concentric zones and grows on dead wood.

JEW'S EAR *Auricularia auricula-judae*

Judas is said to have hanged himself on an elder; the main habitat of this very common fungus sometimes placed in the genus *Hirneola*. Initially cup-shaped and smooth, the fruitbody elongates to the shape of a wrinkled human ear. When moist it is soft, gelatinous and date-brown but it dries smaller, darker and hard. The upper (outer) surface is slightly velvety. It is attached laterally by a small stalk.

Size 2-7 cm across and 2-5 cm broad.
Habitat Mostly on living or dead wood of elder. Also on other trees e.g. beech and sycamore.
Season Throughout the year, softening after rain.
Edible Best in soups or stews; not easily fried.
Similar species *A. mesenterica* (Tripe Fungus) is like a small hairy bracket above but is gelatinous below.

203

YELLOW BRAIN FUNGUS _Tremella mesenterica_

This curious fungus is easy to spot after wet weather with its bright yellow-orange colour and very soft, shiny, irregularly folded, gelatinous fruitbody. Originally disc-like it soon becomes more brain-shaped. Attached to pieces of dead wood by a relatively small basal area; when knocked it wobbles like jelly. In dry weather it shrinks, darkens, becomes very hard and is more difficult to find.

Size	2-8 cm across.
Habitat	On dead twigs and branches of broad-leaved trees, especially hazel, birch and ash. Also on gorse.
Season	All year but more frequent in winter.
Inedible	Insubstantial, with an odd texture.
Similar species	_T. foliacea_ is date-brown and has leaf-like, undulating lobes.

WITCH'S BUTTER *Exidia glandulosa*

When growing on fallen branches the gelatinous black fruitbody is disc- or top-shaped and attached by a short stalk; on erect branches it is more bracket-like and stalkless. It becomes lobed and brain-like when mature. The upper side is roughened with tiny warts, the sides and lower surface are slightly downy. It shrinks to a hard black crust when dry. Also known as *Exidia truncata*.

Size	1-5 cm across.
Habitat	Grouped on dead wood, including stumps of broad-leaved trees; most frequent on oak.
Season	Throughout the year.
Inedible	It has an odd, slippery texture.
Similar species	The firmer Black Bulgar (p.237) leaves a black mark when rubbed with a finger.

205

ORANGE JELLY *Dacrymyces stillatus*

Each rounded, soft fruitbody is only a few mm across but this species grows in large groups and is easily seen. Neighbouring fruitbodies often merge. It occurs as both an orange and a paler yellow form. When old it dries harder and darker.

Size	2-5 mm across.
Habitat	On dead wood of both broad-leaved and coniferous trees. Especially common on wooden gates and fence-posts.
Season	Throughout the year.
Inedible	Insubstantial.
Similar species	Orange Jelly can be confused with Coral Spot (p.248) which also produces many tiny rounded fruitbodies on dead wood. These are dry, warty and pink or dark-red; not orange.

YELLOW FINGERS *Calocera cornea*

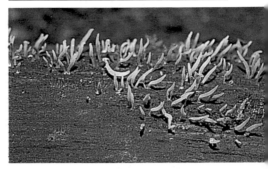

Gelatinous in texture, the tiny pale yellow, smooth, cylindrical fruitbodies have rounded or pointed ends. Most are simple and finger-like but some branch near the apex. Shiny when moist, they are erect and usually gregarious; growing in lines or as groups of 4 or 5 together in a hand-like cluster.

Size	2-10 mm high x 1-2 mm wide.
Habitat	On dead wood of trunks and branches of broad-leaved trees, especially where the bark has been lost. Commonest on beech and oak.
Season	Throughout the year.
Inedible	Insubstantial and surprisingly tough.
Similar species	*C. furcata* is externally very similar but it grows on dead conifers. See Yellow Clubs (p.208)

○ YELLOW CLUBS *Calocera pallidospathulata*

This species is rarely mentioned in older books on fungal identification because it is a relative newcomer to Great Britain; the first record, near Pickering, was in 1969. It is now very common, however, especially in conifer plantations where it frequently takes the place of Yellow Fingers from which it differs in having a larger, stalked, more flattened, club-shaped fruitbody.

Size	5-15 mm high x 2-4 mm wide.
Habitat	Gregarious on dead conifer wood, especially on spruce.
Season	Throughout the year.
Inedible	Slimy texture.
Similar species	The thinner, smaller Yellow Fingers (p.207) grows on dead wood of broad-leaved trees.

JELLY ANTLER FUNGUS *Calocera viscosa*

This beautiful, bright golden-yellow to orange fungus has a gelatinous, tough texture and is smooth and shiny when moist. Firmly rooted in the dead wood from which it grows, the base is paler, flattened and frequently fused with neighbouring fruitbodies. The forked cylindrical branches end in pointed tips which are sometimes further branched, as in antlers.

Size	3-8 cm high, 2-3 cm wide.
Habitat	On stumps and dead roots of conifers, most frequent on pine.
Season	Autumn.
Inedible	Tough and tasteless.
Similar species	Other *Calocera* species are smaller and less branched. Coral Fungi (pp.175 & 176) are dry and brittle.

GIANT PUFFBALL *Langermannia gigantea*

This is our largest fungus, similar in size and shape to a football. The solid young fruitbodies have a thin, white, smooth, dry skin which later turns olive and finally brown when it splits open. The mushroom-smelling flesh is white and firm but turns olive-yellow and later brown as the spores develop.

Size	20-75 cm diameter when mature.
Habitat	Occasional in pasture, woods and gardens; often with nettles on rubbish tips. In groups; forms rings.
Season	Early summer to autumn. Old ones persist.
Edible	When still white inside it is excellent; best baked or fried with lemon juice to add flavour.
Similar species	See Mosaic Puffball (p.211).

MOSAIC PUFFBALL *Calvatia utriformis*

This puffball is the size of a large tennis ball; with a flattened top and a two-layered skin. The rough white outer skin cracks into pyramid-shaped warts but these soon disappear to reveal a white inner skin patterned with a honeycomb-like mosaic. Later smooth and brown, when a hole appears and the edges spread back to release the brown spores. The leathery non-fertile base persists like a thick saucer.

Size 5-15 cm diameter.
Habitat In small groups on unimproved upland pasture. More frequent in the north.
Season Summer to autumn. Brown basal region persists.
Edible The inner flesh must be still white.
Similar species Small specimens of Giant Puffball (p.210) have a single smooth skin and no infertile base.

PESTLE PUFFBALL *Calvatia excipuliformis*

This has a long thick stalk region below the spherical apex giving it a pestle or drum-stick shape. The white flesh is protected by a creamy-brown skin covered with tiny spines and granules. These are soon lost revealing the brown, parchment-like inner skin which splits at the apex and peels open, releasing brown spores. The non-fertile, wrinkled stalk region persists after the spores have been shed.

Size	8-15 cm high, apex 5-10 cm, stalk 3-5 cm across.
Habitat	In parkland, open broad-leaved woodland and on heaths. Occasional; solitary or in small groups.
Season	Late summer to autumn.
Edible	Young specimens are edible.
Similar species	See Common Puffball (p.213).

COMMON PUFFBALL *Lycoperdon perlatum*

The globular head region is often flattened but narrows abruptly to a stem region which is about half the total height. Initially the skin is covered in conical warts (especially on the head region) but these fall off leaving a mesh-like pattern on a brown paper-like skin. This ruptures to form a small apical pore through which the spores escape. Young specimens are firm and white inside.

Size	2-5 cm diameter, 3-8 cm tall.
Habitat	Among leaf litter of both broad-leaved and coniferous woods. Usually gregarious.
Season	Late summer to autumn.
Edible	Only edible when firm and young.
Similar species	Stump Puffball (p.216) grows on wood.

STINKING PUFFBALL *Lycoperdon foetidum*

Shaped like a rounded spinning top, it differs when young from Common Puffball (p.213) in being covered with pale brown, short spines; groups of which converge like wigwam poles. These later fall off leaving a mesh-like pattern on a brown background. Initially firm and white inside it becomes olive-brown as the spores mature and are released through a small apical pore. It has an unpleasant odour when young.

Size	2-5 cm diameter, 2-4 cm high.
Habitat	Frequent in acid woodlands and heaths.
Season	Summer to autumn.
Inedible	Unpleasant smell is offputting.
Similar species	Spiny Puffball (p.215) has longer spines and a darker spore mass. See Common Puffball (p.213)

SPINY PUFFBALL *Lycoperdon echinatum*

Stinking Puffball (p.214) is often wrongly recorded as Spiny Puffball which is pear-shaped with a globular apex and short conical stalk. Even young specimens are dark and densely covered with long brown spines, groups of which curve and fuse at the top to form little pyramids (3-4 mm high). These later fall off leaving a net-like pattern on the dark brown skin. At maturity the spore mass becomes dark brown. A small round pore opens at the apex.

Size	2-6 cm diameter, 3-7 cm high.
Habitat	In broad-leaved woods (e.g. beech) on chalk.
Season	Late summer to autumn.
Inedible	Not worth eating.
Similar species	See Stinking Puffball (p.214).

STUMP PUFFBALL *Lycoperdon pyriforme*

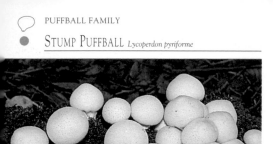

The only puffball which grows in large clusters on rotting wood (This includes dead roots, when it appears to grow on soil). Pear-shaped, and often attached by white strands, it starts granular and creamy-white but matures smooth and ochre-brown when a small hole opens at the apex. When young the inside is firm and white; the upper area turns olive-brown as the spores mature.

Size	1-4 cm diameter, 1-6 cm high.
Habitat	Clustered on rotting wood of both broad-leaved and coniferous trees. Very common.
Season	Summer to late autumn. Old ones persist.
Edible	Can be eaten young but has an unpleasant odour.
Similar species	None. Our other puffballs grow on soil.

MEMBRANOUS PUFFBALL *Vascellum pratense*

One of the commonest puffballs in short grass, it is broadly pear-shaped and flattened at the apex. It is often wider than it is tall and the base is barely narrower. When young the white skin is granular but the granules wash off in the rain leaving a smooth, pale brown surface. Inside, the olive-brown spore mass is clearly separated from the white lower non-fertile region by a membrane. The spores escape through a large apical hole.

Size	2-5 cm diameter, 2-4 cm high.
Habitat	Gregarious in lawns, heaths and near the sea.
Season	Summer to autumn. Lower region persists.
Edible	Only edible when the flesh is white.
Similar species	The distinct membrane between the fertile and non-fertile region prevents confusion.

ROLLING PUFFBALL *Bovista plumbea*

The size and shape of a small golf ball, the smooth white outer skin splits and falls away revealing a thin, lead-grey (hence *plumbea*), parchment-like inner skin. This matures dark brown and peels open revealing the red-brown spore mass which fills the entire fruitbody. When young the inside is firm and white. The fruitbody is attached to the ground at a very small point of contact. Older ones become detached and roll around.

Size	2-4 cm diameter.
Habitat	Short grass including golf courses.
Season	Late summer to autumn.
Edible	Young ones provide a mouthful each.
Similar species	The larger *B. nigrescens* matures a shiny purple-black. More common in the North.

COMMON EARTHBALL *Scleroderma citrinum*

Spherical or slightly flattened, Common Earthball may become slightly lobed. The tiny stalk-like region is often buried in the soil. The yellow-brown, thick (to 5 mm), scaly skin has a reptilian appearance and finally ruptures to release the spores. Initially white, the inside is soon purple-black with white streaks and finally develops into a powdery brown spore mass. It has a rubbery smell.

Size	3-10 cm diameter.
Habitat	On the ground near trees, especially birch and oak; prefers acid soils. Even grows in pavements.
Season	Summer to autumn. Old ones persist a few months.
Poisonous	Causes gastric upset especially if undercooked.
Similar species	See Smooth Earthball (p.220).

SMOOTH EARTHBALL *Scleroderma verrucosum*

This has a more pear-shaped fruitbody which has a distinct grooved, stalk-like base attached to white threads. The tough, leathery skin is thinner (2-3 mm) than that of Common Earthball and has much finer, brown scales (these are lost in old specimens). The skin ruptures near the apex to produce an irregularly-shaped opening. Initially white then dark brown and marbled, the inside finally develops into a brown spore mass. The smell is indistinct.

Size	3-5 cm diameter, 6-7 cm high.
Habitat	On acid soils in woods and on heathland.
Season	Summer to autumn.
Poisonous	Not deadly but can cause diarrhoea.
Similar species	See Common Earthball (p.219). Puffballs (pp. 210-218) have thinner, softer skins.

STINKHORN *Phallus impudicus*

Also known as Witch's Egg, this fungus feels soft due to a jelly-like layer just beneath the skin. This later splits at the apex and a thick, white hollow stem emerges with the texture of polystyrene and bearing a wrinkled, conical, slimy olive-green head topped by a small white ring. At this stage the fungus smells like bad drains and attracts flies which eat the spore-bearing slime leaving a white honeycomb top.

Size	'Egg' 3-5 cm diameter. Mature 10-20 cm x 2-3 cm.
Habitat	Among leaf litter in woodlands, also in gardens.
Season	Early summer to late autumn.
Edible	The egg stage (before it smells) can be eaten.
Similar species	*P.hadriani* has a pink egg. The egg stage is extremely like a puffball.

DOG STINKHORN *Mutinus caninus*

Less common than Stinkhorn but still frequent, the Dog Stinkhorn is much smaller and the more elongated white egg stage is tinged pale brown. The slim, brittle polystyrene-like stem is white in the lower regions but dark orange near the apex which bears the pointed, dark olive, slimy spore mass. A mildly unpleasant smell attracts flies which eat the spore layer leaving a dark orange honeycomb at the tip.

Size	'Egg' 2-3 cm diameter, Mature 4-8 cm x 1 cm.
Habitat	In woodland leaf litter and around rotting wood.
Season	Summer to autumn.
Inedible	The egg is too small to be worthwhile.
Similar species	The small size and orange tip distinguishes it from Stinkhorn (p.221).

COLLARED EARTHSTAR *Geastrum triplex*

Earthstars are like puffballs with an outer skin which splits and peels back. None are common but this one is locally frequent. Initially like a pointed puffball, the thick (to 5 mm), fleshy outer skin splits into 5 or 6 creamy-brown lobes which open flat in a star-like pattern. The base of each lobe splits to form a raised circular collar. This surrounds the thin-skinned inner bag which has a small fringed apical opening through which the spores escape.

Size	4-7 cm diameter (when fully open).
Habitat	In leaf litter under beech on chalk soils.
Season	Late summer to autumn.
Inedible	Tough and full of spores.
Similar	The flesh-coloured *G. rufescens* lacks a collar.
species	*G. pectinatum* has a stalked inner bag.

223

BIRD'S NEST FUNGUS *Cyathus striatus*

Bird's Nest fungi are very small. This is the commonest with a deeply cup-shaped fruitbody, the opening of which is initially covered by a white skin that ruptures to reveal a group of tiny, grey, egg-shaped sacs (peridioles) containing the spores. Each is attached by a thin thread. The inner surface of the 'nest' is grooved and grey. The outer surface is red-brown and bristly.

Size	1.5 cm tall, 1 cm diameter.
Habitat	On dead twigs, needles and bark fragments.
Season	Summer to early autumn.
Inedible	Tough and tiny.
Similar species	The rarer *C. olla* has a smooth outer side and a trumpet-shaped top. *Crucibulum laeve* has smooth, straight-edged 'nests'.

ORANGE PEEL FUNGUS *Aleuria aurantia*

At a casual glance this looks like a piece of orange peel. Initially bowl-like, the thin-fleshed, fragile fruitbody expands to a saucer-shape and may flatten but it has an irregular, undulating margin which is frequently split. The inner, spore-bearing surface is smooth and bright orange; outer surface is minutely downy and paler. There is no stalk.

Size	2-8 cm diameter.
Habitat	Gregarious on damp bare soil, occasionally among herbs in shady places. Commonest on woodland rides, ditch banks and in gardens.
Season	Autumn to early winter.
Edible	Needs cooking; bland flavour.
Similar species	The red *Sarcoscypha coccinea* grows on hazel twigs.

LEMON PEEL FUNGUS *Otidea onotica*

Young fruitbodies start saucer-shaped but one side develops faster causing it to elongate, split and curl inwards. This gives rise to an alternative name - Hare's Ear, which confusingly is also used for the related *O. leporina* (see below). The ochre-yellow outer surface is smooth. The short white stalk region is usually buried in soil.

Size	2-5 cm across, 4-10 cm high.
Habitat	Gregarious among leaf litter or moss under beech or oak. Occasional.
Season	Summer to autumn.
Edible	Insubstantial and not recommended.
Similar species	*O. leporina* is darker brown and lacks pink tints. Species of *Flavoscypha* are brighter yellow.

PIG'S EARS *Peziza badia*

The genus *Peziza* contains many medium-sized, thin and fragile species with a cup or saucer-shaped fruitbody and little or no stalk. *P. badia* is one of the largest and the undulating, irregular fruitbody lacks a stalk. The smooth, inner spore-bearing surface is dark olive-brown; outer is slightly scurfy near the margin and deep red-brown.

Size	3-8 cm diameter.
Habitat	Gregarious on moist acid soil, especially on paths and ditch banks.
Season	Late summer to autumn.
Poisonous	Especially if eaten raw.
Similar species	Most other *Peziza* species are a paler colour on one or both surfaces. See pp. 228 & 229.

LARGE CUP FUNGUS *Peziza repanda*

Much paler than the previous species, this has large shallow, saucer-like fruitbodies and an undulating margin which is frequently split, giving a toothed appearance. There is no stalk. The smooth inner spore-bearing surface is a pale chestnut-brown; contrasting with the pale cream of the scurfy outer surface.

Size	3-12 cm diameter.
Habitat	On the ground, often close to rotting stumps and also on sawdust.
Season	Early summer to autumn.
Inedible	Related species are poisonous.
Similar species	The fawn-coloured Straw Cup Fungus (p.229) is most easily separated by its habitat. *P. succosa* is darker brown and exudes a yellow juice when broken.

STRAW CUP FUNGUS *Peziza vesiculosa*

The young fruitbody is deeply cup-shaped with only a small central opening but this enlarges as the fungus grows. The margins remain inrolled but become split, resulting in a ragged appearance. The inner surface is pale brown, smooth but wrinkled ; the outer side is scurfy and pale buff. Neighbouring fruitbodies often fuse to form large clusters.

Size	3-8 cm diameter.
Habitat	Old straw bales, manure, horse dung, cultivated mushroom beds, compost heaps and rich soil.
Season	Throughout the year.
Poisonous	Edible if well-cooked but not recommended.
Similar species	The smaller *P. cerea* grows on damp mortar and soil and is common in poorly ventilated cellars.

EYELASH FUNGUS *Scutellinia scutellata*

The flattened, saucer-like fruitbody is much smaller than those of the *Peziza* genus but the clustered nature and scarlet colour of Eyelash Fungus make it easy to find. Starting knob-like then saucer-shaped, the fruitbody finally flattens but maintains a small upturned margin. The bright scarlet, smooth inner surface contrasts with the brown bristly hairs of the outer side; these project above the margin like eyelashes. There is no stalk.

Size	0.5-1.5 cm diameter.
Habitat	Clustered on damp rotting wood and on damp soil.
Season	Spring to late autumn.
Inedible	Insubstantial.
Similar species	Several closely related species are only separated by microscopic features.

WHITE SADDLE *Helvella crispa*

This odd-looking fungus has a saddle-shaped cap with two or three undulating, irregular lobes and margins free of the stalk. The upper spore-bearing surface is creamy-white; the lower surface is pale ochre and slightly downy. The stem is brittle, white and internally chambered with deep longitudinal surface furrows, some of which fork and reunite.

Size Cap 2-6 cm, stem 4-7 cm x 2-4 cm.

Habitat Under broad-leaved trees and beside woodland paths.

Season Summer to autumn.

Poisonous Can cause gastric upset, especially if eaten raw.

Similar species Elfin's Saddle (p.232) has a dark grey, more convoluted cap. Common Morel (p.234) has a brain-like cap and a smooth stem.

ELFIN'S SADDLE *Helvella lacunosa*

This is like a dark-coloured version of the preceding species. The cap is more convoluted and the irregular lobes have rounded margins which are attached to the stem, resulting in hollow chambers. The cap is dark grey to black on the outside and a similar colour within the chambers. The grey-brown hollow stalk is deeply furrowed and has numerous cross walls.

Size	Cap 2-4 cm, stem 2-5 cm x 1-2 cm.
Habitat	On sandy or burnt ground under both coniferous and broad-leaved trees.
Season	Summer to autumn.
Poisonous	Can cause gastric upset so best avoided.
Similar species	White Saddle (p.231) is much paler and the cap lobes are free of the stem.

TURBAN FUNGUS *Gyromitra esculenta*

Also known as False Morel, this is uncommon in Britain but can be mistaken for Morel (p.234) and is deadly poisonous. The broad, fist-shaped, deeply lobed, brain-like, red-brown cap is divided internally into a number of hollow chambers. The short creamy-brown stem is externally furrowed and internally hollowed into several chambers. It is fragile in texture.

Size	Cap 5-15 cm, stem 2-5 cm x 2-3 cm.
Habitat	In coniferous woods. Less rare in Scotland.
Season	Spring to early summer.
Poisonous	Can be fatal and even when consumed after careful preparation is suspected of causing cancer.
Similar species	See Common Morel (p.234).

COMMON MOREL *Morchella esculenta*

The hollow egg-shaped cap may be globular or more conical and is often not symmetrical. The deeply pitted surface is like honeycomb and the pits vary from pale brown to grey; darker when old. The pale ochre stem is grooved near its base and has a single hollow chamber.

Size	Cap 3-8 cm across, stem 3-8 cm x 1.5-2.5 cm.
Habitat	On well-drained soil, usually under broad-leaved trees in woodland edges, hedgerows and gardens.
Season	April to May with a short fruiting season.
Edible	Wonderful flavour and texture. Dries well.
Similar species	*M. elata* has a pointed conical cap with the pits in vertical rows. See Turban Fungus (p.233).

JELLY BABIES *Leotia lubrica*

A distinctive little fungus with a slippery, gelatinous feel, its rounded olive-yellow cap becomes flat and centrally depressed but with inrolled lobed margins and a smooth underside. The pale yellow stem is slightly flattened and flecked with tiny green specks.

Size Cap 1-1.5 cm across, stem 2-5 cm x 4-7 mm.
Habitat In moist bare ground and among moss under broad-leaved trees, especially beech.
Season Late summer to autumn.
Inedible Insubstantial.
Similar species The rare *Spathularia flavida* is bright yellow and grows under conifers. *Mitrula paludosa*, which grows in waterlogged leaf litter, has a club-shaped, orange head and a slender white stem.

○ GREEN WOOD CUP *Chlorosplenium aeruginascens*

Wood which has been stained blue-green by the action of this fungus is commonly found; the fruitbodies are rarer. Initially goblet-shaped with a short stalk, the top becomes saucer-shaped and later irregularly wavy. The smooth upper surface is bright blue-green; the outer surface and stalk start paler but mature blue-green. It is soft in texture. Also known as *Chlorociboria aeruginascens*.

Size	0.5-1.0 cm diameter.
Habitat	On dead wood of broad-leaved trees e.g. oak.
Season	From spring to autumn.
Inedible	The stained wood is part of the intricate patterns employed in Tunbridge ware.
Similar species	None.

Black Bulgar *Bulgaria inquinans*

This species has a firm rubbery consistency. Top-shaped with inrolled margins, it later flattens to become more like a thick button with a concave, shiny black upper surface which leaves a black mark when rubbed with a finger. The outer surface is scurfy and dark brown. In dry conditions the shrunken fruitbody has a leathery feel.

Size	1-3 cm diameter, 1-1.5 cm high.
Habitat	Gregarious, sometimes clustered. Grows from the bark of fallen trunks, mostly of oak and sweet chestnut.
Season	Autumn and into early winter.
Inedible	Like eating rubber!
Similar species	Witch's Butter (p.205) is less firm, has a warty surface and does not leave a black mark.

237

○ PURPLE JELLY FUNGUS *Ascocoryne sarcoides*

The soft jelly-like consistency is similar to that of the basidiomycete Jelly Fungi (pp.203-209). The tiny purple-pink, spherical fruitbody becomes more like an inverted cone with a smooth flat disc or saucer-shaped top and a very short stalk. The disc edges are wavy and frequently distorted by the proximity of neighbouring fruitbodies. *Coryne sarcoides* indicates the similar asexual stage.

Size	0.5-1.5 cm diameter.
Habitat	Gregarious. Clustered on barkless dead wood of broad-leaved trees, especially beech.
Season	Most frequent in autumn and winter.
Inedible	Insubstantial.
Similar species	*A. cylichnium* has larger spores. *Neobulgaria* pura is a pale flesh colour.

Shaggy Earth Tongue *Trichoglossum hirsutum*

The dark brown to black fruitbody is not much bigger than a matchstick. It is club-shaped with a smooth, flattened, tongue-like fertile head region which narrows abruptly to a more cylindrical, velvety stem.

Size	3-8 cm tall.
Habitat	Among moss in wet acid grassland and especially with bog moss (*Sphagnum*).
Season	Late summer to autumn.
Inedible	Insubstantial.
Similar species	On sandy soils the Smooth Earth Tongue (*Geoglossum cookeianum*) is smaller, with a less distinct head region and smooth stem. The rare Green Earth Tongue (*Microglossum viride*) grows in moss under trees.

SCARLET CATERPILLAR FUNGUS *Cordyceps militaris*

The tiny finger-like fruitbodies stand out because of their bright colour. The lower part is cylindrical, smooth and curving; it merges into the slightly broader, rough-surfaced, fertile apex. It grows from a buried dead caterpillar or pupa.

Size	2-5 cm high, 0.5 cm wide.
Habitat	Solitary or in small groups emerging from a buried butterfly larva or pupa which the fungus has killed. In grassland or among woodland leaf litter.
Season	Late summer to late autumn.
Inedible	Used as a Chinese 'herbal' medicine.
Similar species	The yellow-brown *C.ophioglossoides* parasitises the False Truffle (p.243). See also the smooth-surfaced Orange Clubs (p.174).

ERGOT *Claviceps purpurea*

Autumnal inspection of grass flower heads may reveal a small, brown-black, hard, banana-shaped object. This Ergot sclerotium (resting stage) falls to the ground and produces tiny, drumstick-shaped fruitbodies in spring (see inset). These bear sticky spores which infect grasses (and cereals) via their stigmas and take over the flower to produce a sclerotium. The cause of ergotism from contaminated flour.

Size	Sclerotium varies with host: 5-20 mm x 2-4 mm.
Habitat	On the flowers of grasses and cereals.
Season	Late summer to autumn.
Poisonous	Used medicinally to prevent haemorrhage after childbirth and to ease migraine.
Similar species	None.

SUMMER TRUFFLE *Tuber aestivum*

Although not as prized as those found in France and Italy, this used to be collected by professionals and their dogs. It is about the size, shape and colour of a squash ball but covered with pyramidal-shaped warts, thus looking like a rounded pine cone. The inside is pale brown, marbled white, with a strong but pleasant smell and a nutty taste.

Size	3-7 cm in diameter.
Habitat	Buried in the ground under broad-leaved trees; mostly under beech on chalky soil.
Season	Summer to autumn.
Edible	Small amounts are used as flavouring.
Similar species	The smaller Winter Truffle (*T. brumale*) has grey marbled flesh. Black Truffle (*T. melanosporum*) has grooved polygonal warts but is not found in Britain.

FALSE TRUFFLE *Elaphomyces granulatus*

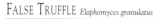

This is perhaps the most frequently found of the subterranean fungi especially as it is often parasitised by the club-shaped fungus *Cordyceps ophioglossoides* which emerges above ground. Firm and about the size and shape of a large marble, its thick warty, red-brown skin surrounds the flecked, purple-brown flesh which darkens as the spores mature. It has no distinctive smell.

Size	2-4 cm diameter.
Habitat	Just below the surface in woodland soil; most frequent in conifer woods, especially with pine.
Season	Throughout the year.
Inedible	Has been used to adulterate edible truffles.
Similar species	The Red Truffle (*Tuber rufum*) has a redder, almost smooth skin.

● CANDLE SNUFF FUNGUS *Xylaria hypoxylon*

One of the commonest wood-rotting fungi. The small, erect, tough fruitbody is simple and finger-shaped or more often strap-like and forked at its apex giving it an antler shape. It is also known as Stag's Horn Fungus. Typically black and downy near the base but grey-white on the upper regions; it becomes all black and warty during the winter.

Size	3-5 cm high, stalk region 2-5 mm wide.
Habitat	Dead wood, especially on rotting stumps of broad-leaved trees. Rarely on conifers.
Season	Throughout the year.
Inedible	It is very tough.
Similar species	*X. carpophyla* is more slender, less branched and grows among leaf litter on old beech fruits.

DEAD MAN'S FINGERS *Xylaria polymorpha*

As its name implies, the clusters of hard, warty, finger-like fruitbodies are distinctly macabre in appearance. Initially grey-brown or brown, the upper region is swollen, flattened and occasionally lobed; it tapers to a short, similar-coloured stalk region. The inside is firm and white under the black outer, spore-bearing layer.

Size	3-7 cm high, 1-3 cm wide.
Habitat	On or around old beech stumps.
Season	Summer through to spring. Old ones persist.
Inedible	Very hard.
Similar species	*X. longipes* has much more slender cylindrical fruitbodies. It grows from buried dead branches of broad-leaved trees, especially sycamore.

KING ALFRED'S CAKES *Daldinia concentrica*

Old fruitbodies are hard, black, light in weight and shiny, looking like burnt cakes. When cut open they reveal concentric light and dark zones, similar to charcoal. When young they are red-brown, heavy and have a matt surface. They are hemispherical or cushion-shaped; often lobed but stalkless, the fruitbody being attached by a broad, flat area.

Size	2-7 cm across.
Habitat	Attached to dead wood of broad-leaved trees; mostly on ash and beech.
Season	Summer to autumn. Old ones persist for many years.
Inedible	A folk remedy to relieve night cramps and is called Cramp Balls for this reason.
Similar species	*Ustulina deusta* forms grey-black crusts on dead stumps especially of beech.

BEECH BARK SPOT _Diatrype disciformis_

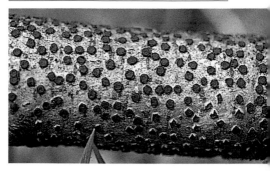

Common, but often overlooked, on beech where the tiny, hard, dark brown to black circular or polygonal disc-shaped fruitbodies burst through the bark. Hundreds together make a regular pattern and darken the colour of the bark. A lens reveals that the flat upper surface of the disc is roughened.

Size	2-3 mm diameter.
Habitat	Gregarious and pushing through the bark of small dead branches of beech. Rare on other broad-leaved trees.
Season	Throughout the year.
Inedible	Mostly buried in bark.
Similar species	_Melogramma bulliardii_ forms grey discs on the bark of hazel and birch. _Hypoxylon fragiforme_ produces small, brown hard lumps on beech.

CORAL SPOT *Nectria cinnabarina*

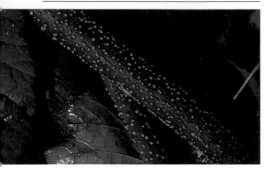

Gregarious on small dead twigs or other wood where the hundreds of minute, cushion-like, dry fruitbodies may almost cover the surface. Most commonly found is the pale orange-pink, non-sexual form which is strictly known as *Tubercularia vulgaris*. The true sexual form is dark red or red-brown with a bumpy surface. Both forms occasionally grow together.

Size	0.5-1.0 mm diameter.
Habitat	Usually on dead branches and twigs of broad-leaved trees and shrubs. Often on wood piles.
Season	Throughout the year.
Inedible	Insubstantial.
Similar species	Orange Jelly (p.206) produces hundreds of tiny fruitbodies on dead wood but when fresh these are very soft and orange in colour.

INDEX OF LATIN NAMES

Bracketed numbers refer to species mentioned in the text but not illustrated.

249

INDEX OF ENGLISH NAMES

255